REDISCOVERING GOD

Are You Stone Deaf To The Spirit or REDISCOVERING GOD?

R T Kendall

Christian Focus Publications

© R. T. Kendall
ISBN 1 85792 072 4

Published in 1994, reprinted in 1999, 2000
by
Christian Focus Publications, Geanies House,
Fearn, Ross-shire, IV20 1TW, Great Britain.

www.christianfocus.com

Cover design by Owen Daily

Abbreviations
NIV - New International Version
AV - Authorised Version

Printed and bound in Great Britain by
Cox & Wyman, Reading, Berkshire

Contents

To
Michael and Jenny

PREFACE

This was my third book with Christian Focus. I have since had several more books published by their press. These people have honoured me by taking me as I am. I have enjoyed my relationship with them, especially with my editor Malcolm Maclean, and I thank all of them for their confidence. I want to thank Alison Walley who has worked through the original typescripts to make them more readable.

This book is an extract from my Friday evening Bible studies at Westminster Chapel on Hebrews that lasted for a little over ten years. Perhaps one day these studies will be published in their entirety. In the meantime, however, it seems to me that there is an urgent need that the issues this book raises be faced. It is my exposition of Hebrews 5:11-6:20, which took place from October 1982 to January 1984.

I am indebted to my friend Lyndon Bowring who suggested the title for this book. He is always helping me with sermon titles! (And yet it was his wife Celia who suggested the title *Meekness and Majesty*, my first book with Christian Focus.) This title succinctly embraces and summarises the double themes of dreadful warning and glorious encouragement.

During the time my Friday series was on Galatians (from 1977 to 1981) Michael Eaton was a regular attender. I hardly knew him then. Years later I was to learn that my treatment of Galatians was a blessing to him. But I was not prepared for the affirmation he gave me when he read my sermons on James and Hebrews 6, after he moved to Johannesburg, South Africa. I cannot adequately express the encouragement I felt when he not only supported me but helped me grasp far more than I myself had seen!

Michael has read what follows, made suggestions, especially by helping me write part of the Introduction. It is with joy and gratitude that I dedicate this book to Dr and Mrs Michael Eaton who now minister at the Chrisco Church in Nairobi, Kenya.

R T Kendall

INTRODUCTION

Would you like to discover God *all over again*? This book, largely an exposition of Hebrews 6, is designed to help you not only to rediscover God for yourself, but to find him more real to you than you ever dreamed possible.

I was converted at the age of six—on Easter Sunday April 5th 1942. I was brought up in a Christian home. I was blessed with godly parents—pillars in my old church, in Ashland, Kentucky. Years later—when I was fifteen, during a 'camp meeting' in Kentucky, while kneeling beside my bed God came to me in a fresh way which I will never forget.

But on October 31st 1955 something very wonderful indeed happened to me. It was while I was a student at Trevecca Nazarene College in Nashville, Tennessee, but also pastor of a church in Palmer, Tennessee, that I was to experience what I now believe is described in various ways in the Epistle to the Hebrews.

What happened was this. I was returning to Nashville on a Monday morning. I decided to spend the whole time in prayer. I had been going through a period of (what seemed at the time) intense suffering. The burden—a terrific anxiety —seized me as I began to pray. God felt a million miles away. Suddenly I perceived (not with my naked eye, although it could not have been more real) that Jesus was literally praying for me at the right hand of God. I was overwhelmed with his love and saw that he cared more for me than I did myself! From that moment, for over an hour, I became a spectator. By the time I arrived at college in Nashville I was a changed man. I entered into a rest of soul—a peace impossible to describe—that even changed the theology I had been taught.

This book is not written to change the reader's theology, for example, regarding the teaching 'once saved, always saved'; or even to my interpretation of Hebrews 6. For all I know, you

9

already believe virtually all I now put forward. What I want this book to do for you is to give you a hunger for more of God than you have ever had—with the hope that your life will be transformed afresh.

Hebrews 6:4-6 has been a theological battleground for nearly 2,000 years. You may or may not be convinced of the position I take; the more important section begins with Hebrews 6:9 in any case. But I hope you will see, if you find yourself a bit discouraged (as those Hebrew Christians were) and if you find yourself 'dull of hearing', thus are not hearing God clearly (like those Hebrew Christians), that there is a way forward. And yet the reader ought not to begin with the exposition of Hebrews 6:9 without seeing it in its awesome context. Please read through the preceding section right from the beginning, even if it seems tedious at times; the reward, I believe, is worth pursuing.

What I envisage for you is not necessarily a crisis experience like I described above. I myself have enjoyed much more since then over the years—what Paul calls being changed from glory to glory (2 Cor. 3:18). I also know what it is to lose a lot of the joy I had—mostly owing to bitterness. Finding my way back has come through knowing how to forgive, to dignify the trials and to remain open to the Holy Spirit.

What I hope you will discover is two things. First, to find that you can be used of God to exceed anything you dreamed possible (Eph. 3:20). It also means that you can be renewed again to a change of mind whereby the Lord Jesus will become more real and precious than ever. Secondly, that you will see Abraham as the model for great spiritual growth and insights. He was Paul's model for justification by faith alone (Rom. 4) and the model which the writer of the Epistle to the Hebrews puts before us with reference to a most unusual awareness of God. The same God swore an oath to Abraham; he may well do it for *you*. That is my prayer for you, the reader.

Although I myself lost a good deal of the joy I described, three things stayed with me which I never lost. First, an infallible assurance that I was eternally saved. Secondly, a robust view of the sovereignty of God. Thirdly, a sense of sin. All three of these were quite new to me. I wondered if I had discovered something new! I was brought right back to my New Testament with an ability to read it non-defensively.

Hebrews 6 however remained a problem. I was far from sure how to handle it.

Why is Hebrews 6 a theological battleground? If you are a Calvinist you are in difficulty. Calvinists teach that saved people cannot fall away. Hebrews 6:6 says otherwise. Arminians are in difficulty. They teach that saved people can fall away but can be restored. Hebrews 6:6 says otherwise.

I well remember a sermon I heard by my mentor Dr N. B. Magruder (the man who later preached my ordination sermon) on Hebrews 6. He stated that Hebrews 6:4-5 are but the 'appearances' of saved people—they are counterfeit, not the real thing. I took that to be the way out. E. W. Johnson made it even plainer: all who have been regenerated have been illuminated but not all who are illuminated have been regenerated. Hebrews 6:4-5, he concluded, were illuminated but not regenerated. My old friend Ernie Reisinger made me a present of the works of John Owen, whose interpretation of Hebrews 6:4-5 (like the above, showing that they were not really saved people) actually motivated me to come to Oxford years later! And yet there was an uneasiness deep inside that I had opted for an intellectually respectable position but which left a lot of questions unanswered.

It was only after I began a detailed study of the Epistle to the Hebrews at Westminster Chapel on Friday nights that I began to feel more and more uneasy. We began studying Hebrews in the spring of 1981. By the end of June 1982 we had reached Hebrews 3:6. Then came our summer break. That summer I read all I could on Hebrews—an unexpected awakening exploded in my mind: Hebrews 6:4-6 means *exactly what it says*! The impossibility of renewed *repentance* was what those who fell away incurred. These people were saved. The descriptions of verses 4 and 5 were anything but counterfeit. What was forfeited was the ability to hear God speak again—which is why there could be no renewal of a change of mind. In a word: Hebrews 6:4-6 describes truly saved people who refused to be open to the Word and the Spirit; as a consequence of this they became stone deaf—a permanent and (sadly) irrevocable condition. No wonder that they could not ever be renewed again to repentance!

In this Introduction I want us to proceed from the general to the particular. In other words, let us take a brief look at the Epistle as a whole before looking at the details.

Let me introduce Hebrews like this. For we know that when Christians discuss whether one can lose salvation, Hebrews chapter 6 gets mentioned every time.

When a preacher opens a meeting for a time of questions, the chances are high that one of them will be about Hebrews chapter 6.

When a young person happens to be with his pastor or vicar and has an opportunity to ask a question, he will often say, 'Pastor, there is one passage of Scripture I've often wondered about ...'. Often you know what is coming before he finishes. He is going to ask a question about Hebrews chapter 6.

With each of the twenty-one letters of the New Testament (Romans to Jude), it is important to read all of them right through from beginning to end. Otherwise you are likely to misunderstand them by taking sentences 'out of context'. If you wrote me a letter, you would not like it if I took a sentence here and a sentence there but never worked through it from beginning to end. What would you think if I wrote back and told you how much I enjoyed one sentence of your letter? 'That really was a wonderful sentence,' I say. But then I add, 'However, there was a sentence in the middle somewhere that I really found difficult.' Then you discover I had never read the letter straight through but had only dipped into it, a sentence here and a sentence there. 'What a silly way to read a letter,' you would say—if it were your letter I was reading!

But many people read the letters of the Bible in precisely that way—and then complain about 'difficult passages'!

It is well-known that you can make the Bible mean anything

you want it to mean if you take a verse here and a verse there and string them together in the way you want to make the point you want. But that is not the right way to read the Bible. I suppose you can read a telephone directory or a dictionary that way, but most forms of writing have to be read through logically from beginning to end. There is a story about the British politician, Winston Churchill, that is interesting in this connection. The story goes like this. He once had a major speech to deliver and knew that his enemies might take phrases 'out of context' and so would easily be able to attack him by twisting what he was saying. He got his secretary to type out every sentence separately on cards, and then mixed them up, so that he could see what each sentence looked like 'out of context'! He knew that any sentence taken out of context could be made to mean almost anything.

The letter to the Hebrews contains the most powerful warnings and the most thrilling encouragement anywhere in the Bible. There are six 'warning passages' in it (2:1-4; 3:7-4:13; 6:4-6; 10:26-39; 12:16-17; 12:25-29). The most famous is Hebrews 6:4-6. The way to understand Hebrews 6:4-6 is to begin at Hebrews 1:1! By the time you get to Hebrews 6:6 it is not so difficult—if you have followed the writer carefully—to see what he means.

Let us begin to read the letter straight through. It begins by laying a foundation concerning who Jesus is, and says eight basic things about him in Hebrews 1:1-4. He is (i) God's last Word to the human race, 1:1-2a, (ii) heir of all things, 1:2b, (iii) creator, 1:2c, (iv) divine, 1:3a, (v) Lord of history and of providence, 1:3b, (vi) one who made purification of sins, 1:3c, (vii) one who is seated in a position of kingship and rule, 1:3d, and (viii) one who is exalted above angels, 1:4.

Then in Hebrews 1:5-14 he makes the same points all over again but this time showing what he has said from the Old Testament. He quotes six passages of Scripture, all of which make the same points he has made in the first four verses. He is saying what he said in Hebrews 1:1-4 again, but now making those same points from the Old Testament.

What a great salvation it is! It is this that leads him into his first warning (Heb. 2:1-4). There are two things about it that are worth noting. (i) It is addressed to Christians. He says 'How shall *we* escape...?' (ii) The warning is about 'neglecting salvation'. He does not say 'How shall *they* escape if *they reject* such a great salvation ...?' He says, 'How shall *we escape* if we *neglect* such a great salvation?' That is the meaning of the word 'neglect'. You *reject* something if you don't want it and will not have it. You *neglect* something if you do have it but don't use it. That is the nature of the warning when it is first issued. It is about Christians 'neglecting' the salvation that they have.

However, the writer moves on and (as with every warning passage) follows up what he has said with the most thrilling encouragement (2:5-18). The writer was speaking about being brought to our inheritance (1:14). Now he says, 'This world to come about which I am writing is not for angels. It is for people!' He goes on to explain. God intended to give the world to people. However, something went wrong and 'we do not yet see' all things put under the feet of men and women. We do not see them crowned with glory and honour. What we see instead is that Jesus made it to glory. Jesus has fulfilled our destiny for us! The only way we can get to glory now is to travel along the pathway he has already travelled. He made it to glory himself and now is willing to 'bring many sons to glory'. He knows how to sustain us. He has suffered. He has been tempted. He knows all about living a godly life in this world. He got himself through to glory and now he can get his 'brothers' through to glory also. We must not 'neglect' salvation. If we persist in faith Jesus will bring us through to honour and reward in the 'world to come' of which he is speaking, the heavenly 'inheritance'.

At Hebrews 3:1-6, the writer develops a new line of thought. Moses was the leader of Israel and at the time of their being redeemed by the Passover lamb he was seeking to lead the Israelites into Canaan. Jesus is similar. He has redeemed us by his blood and is seeking now to lead us into our Canaan. For the Christian there is a spiritual equivalent of a land flowing with milk and honey. But the 'Canaan' of the Christian is greater than Israel's Canaan. Jesus is greater than Moses. Both Moses and Jesus were faithful. Yet the house in which Moses was faithful was the tabernacle. The house over which Jesus is faithful is the entire people of God. We shall have the experience of being Jesus' house, filled with his glory like the tabernacle if we persist in faith (Heb. 3:6b).

This leads the writer into his second warning (Heb. 3:7-4:13). It is his longest and his fullest. We must remember when we get to Hebrews 6 that the writer has already been through Hebrews 3-4. Actually the basic warning of Hebrews 6 has already been said quite clearly before the writer ever gets to Hebrews 6. In Hebrews 6:4-6 he is following up for the third time what he already has said in Hebrews 2:1-4 and Hebrews 3:7- 4:13.

In Hebrews 3:7-4:13 he warns them not to be like the Israelites who were redeemed by the blood of the lamb but, apart from Joshua and Caleb, never got to what they were redeemed for.

Again we note several things about his second warning. It was addressed to Christians. Also, it is about Christians neglecting salvation to such an extent they are *unable* to hear God's voice. He adds some things that he had not said in 2:1-4. It is possible to lose what one was redeemed for. The Israelites never lost being delivered from Egypt by the blood of the lamb. They never went back to Egypt. But they did lose Canaan. One could say: they never went back to what they were redeemed *from*. But they lost what they were redeemed *for*. They lost Canaan by not hearing God's voice. Another point which was not mentioned in 2:1-4 is that there was a specific moment and a definitive point when they lost what they were redeemed for. That was the point (mentioned in Numbers 14:21-23) at which God took an oath and swore that they would never be able to enter Canaan. Before that point they *could* enter Canaan (read Numbers 14:7-9). After that point they could *not* enter Canaan (read Numbers 14:39-45). The point where God took the oath was the crucial point. At that point they 'fell' and could not be renewed to repentance by

Moses or anyone else. They were forgiven (Num. 14:20) but the thing God wanted to give them was lost. What God *had already* given them could not be lost. What God *wanted* to give them could be lost.

Once again the writer follows up his warning with encouragement. He now moves on to the theme of the priesthood of Jesus. He introduces the matter in Hebrews 4:14-16. We do not need to 'fall' as the Israelites fell. We have a great High Priest, he says, Jesus who has gone into heaven for us. He is sympathetic. He gives us mercy to cover our past; he ministers grace to meet the needs of the future.

Then he begins to explain further, in 5:1-10. Old Testament high priests were human and ministered in an earthly sanctuary for various kinds of sins. But they had many weaknesses and limitations. Jesus is a High Priest of a different kind, not a Levite, but a High Priest in a unique order, the order of Melchizedek.

We are now getting close to the famous passage in Hebrews chapter 6 which we wish to study in detail. It actually comes in as a digression. The writer was mentioning Melchizedek (5:10) and wants to say more about that subject. But he turns aside for twenty-four verses (in our Bibles; of course he himself did not have 'verses'). It is this lengthy digression that we want to study. He eventually gets back to where he left off. Hebrews 6:20 speaks again of 'Melchizedek' and he picks up at the end of 6:20 from where he left off at Hebrews 5:10.

He says to them in effect, 'I really want to tell you much more about what it means to live by Jesus as our heavenly Melchizedek. But you have to be really moving on with the Lord for it to make any sense to you. You have to be energetically seeking to live for God. You have to be having all of your spiritual faculties fully working. You have to be pressing on with God. Then the teaching about Jesus as your Melchizedek will make sense to you.'

He says (Heb. 5:11), 'I want to tell you a lot more about this figure in the Scriptures, Melchizedek. But I have a problem. I am not sure whether you are really moving on with the Lord in such a way that you are able to take what I want to give to you. I fear that while I might be telling you all about living on Jesus as your heavenly Melchizedek, you are too deaf spiritually to take in what I shall be saying.' He goes on (Heb. 5:12), 'You have been Christians a long time. By now you ought to be helping others and teaching them what it means to be growing and moving on with God. But instead you seem to have got stuck at a very elementary stage. Even quite simple things about knowing God seem to be difficult for you. You still seem to be at the point where you need milk, but the teaching I want to give you about Melchizedek is not milk; it is meat. It is good food for those who want to move on in the godly life, the life which achieves something for God.'

At this point in this letter, the writer is preparing his friends for the strong teaching he wants to give them. They are Christian people but have become somewhat sluggish. They need to rouse themselves and get ready to grow in grace, as they are led by Jesus, their heavenly Melchizedek. There is one deprivation we must suffer by plunging into Hebrews 5:11-12 (Chapter 1). That is, the teaching concerning God's rest in Hebrews 3 and 4. However, we can summarise the meaning. Entering Canaan, which the ancient Israelites could not do, is what believers today can do: by which we experience incredible peace and the awesome sovereignty of God. It is not Heaven, it is a little bit of Heaven to go to Heaven in! It is promised to every believer. The way forward is described in Hebrews 4:12-16 and elaborated upon in Hebrews 6:9-20, which we will cover in this book.

This Epistle was written while the temple in Jerusalem was still standing. Various references in the Epistle make this clear— proof that it was written prior to 70 AD when the temple was destroyed. So the readers of this Epistle were actually conscious not only that the temple stood—but it thrived! We may ask, what happened to the veil, the curtain, that was ripped in two 'from top to bottom' (Matt. 27:51)? Answer: it was either sewn back together or replaced. The ancient worship was resumed as though Jesus never died on the cross.

Jesus had prophesied that the temple would be destroyed
(Luke 19:44). After thirty years the temple stood and the old
worship continued. This was discouraging to Hebrew Christians
and our Epistle faces this problem. Could Jesus have got it
wrong? Had these Hebrew Christians got it wrong?

'No!' thunders our writer. He shows that Jesus is our great
High Priest—now in Heaven. Never mind that the ancient
temple stands! Jesus' work on the cross is a finished work—he
applies the blood he shed to all who come to God by him (Heb.
7:25). The Epistle is therefore largely about the priesthood of
Christ. What is more, the temple was destroyed shortly after the
Epistle was written!

But it contains most dreadful warnings. That is what my own
book examines. Hebrews also gives us most tender words of
encouragement! That too is what we will look at. It is a timely
word today—for the church generally and all of us as believers
particularly.

Do you fear you are on the scrapheap? Do you fear that the
skeletons in your cupboard prevent you from being used again?
Do you fear that some scandalous sin in your life means you are
in Hebrews 6:6? This book is for you.

What matters is not your past but your present openness to the
Word and the Spirit. I say this not to give false encouragement.
Your openness to the Word and the Holy Spirit proves beyond
any doubt that you are *not* in a Hebrews 6:4-6 situation, but
qualify for the lasting fruit that accompanies salvation (Heb.
6:9).

Despite the awesome warning (which is not hypothetical but
real), I pray that this book will prove to be one of the most
encouraging you have read.

We now move from the general to the particular.

Part One

God's
Requirements
For Spiritual Growth

1

The Problem

We have much to say about this, but it is hard to explain because you are slow to learn. In fact, though by this time you ought to be teachers, you need someone to teach you the elementary truths of God's word all over again. You need milk, not solid food! (Hebrews 5:11-12)

The writer of Hebrews fears for his readers. He knows sadly that something has happened to them. So what does he say to them? He says, 'You need someone to teach you ... all over again'. As I said in the Introduction, this section of Hebrews is regarded by many as the most difficult passage in the Bible. However, I would suggest that 5:12 could be the key to this letter. Instead of being teachers by this time, these Hebrew Christians needed someone to teach them again the ABCs of the oracles of God.

Verse 12 certainly may well be the key to chapter 6, but I wonder if it could also be a key to the whole epistle. The reason I suggest this is that the whole thrust of chapters 3 and 4 is one continuous warning, where the writer refers to the children of Israel in the wilderness, and warns that what happened to them could be repeated with the Hebrew Christians to whom he is writing. So, it was their spiritual state that made him want to write the epistle in the first place.

These Hebrew Christians had stopped short of a fruitful Christian life. What a person does with the light of God, and in obedience to the will of God, will affect his or her own ability to grasp the truth.

We see this in 2 Peter 1:5-6: 'add to your faith goodness; and to goodness, knowledge; and to knowledge, self-control; and to self-control, perseverance; and to perseverance, godliness.' This is Peter's way of saying, Walk in the light. God does not lead us from A to Z, but from A to B and B to C. Then in verse

8, Peter says, 'For if you possess these qualities in increasing measure, they will keep you from being ineffective and unproductive in your knowledge of our Lord Jesus Christ.' And then a verse that is often forgotten (and I am amazed how many commentators wish they did *not* have to deal with 2 Peter 1:9): 'But if anyone does not have them, he is near-sighted and blind, and has forgotten that he *has been cleansed* from his past sins.'

I do not mean to be unfair, but the traditional Calvinist interpretation of Hebrews 6 says that those described in verses 4 through 6 were not really saved. 2 Peter 1:9 describes those who did not have spiritual fruits; some might say they too were not saved. But what *does* Peter say? He says that such a one has forgotten that he was purged from his old sins, *yet he was saved.* What happens is that if a person does not walk in the light, something happens to his faculties. I do not mean his intelligence, his IQ, or his intellectual ability. I mean having a warm heart to grasp God's word, for this is the most important thing of all. The alternative is unthinkable.

The judgment seat of Christ

In many ways, the key to Hebrews is the judgment seat of Christ. That is partly why you have references to the judgment in chapters 9 and 10, as well as all the warnings that appear right through the letter. All believers are going to stand before the judgment seat of Christ.

I think that if there is anything the devil wants, it is to get Christians to think that all that matters is being saved or lost. Yet that is not all there is to it. The same Paul who believed in the imputed righteousness of Christ—that we are saved by faith alone and the blood of Christ covers us and we escape the wrath of God—also believed that we must give an account of the things done in the body. There is a reward or loss to be meted out at the judgment seat of Christ.

Now the writer of Hebrews fears for his readers' loss. Chapter 6:4-6 says that it is apparently too late for some. They are not going to have anything. The writer hopes that he has caught the rest of them in time. And yet he is still worried about them, because he says they have become dull of hearing, and they ought to be teachers by now. He does not want them, this remnant that he addresses, to be in the same position as those that he will describe in chapter 6. So he reminds them of Christ's sacrifice and priestly work, although he knows this subject is too much for them. He wanted so much to say a lot about Melchizedek (v. 11).

I think that verse 12 of chapter 5 is possibly the most underestimated verse by many interpreters of Hebrews. Some expositors merely look at Hebrews 5:12 as a little slap on the wrist, as if the writer was just saying, 'Well you ought to be further along than that. Come on, shape up, let us just have a little more zeal there.' It is seen as a kind of patting them on the back and giving them a little push. But that is not it at all! The writer wants them to see how serious it is.

Let me tell you something very interesting. What chapter, outside this epistle, has the most to say in the New Testament about the judgment seat of Christ? I think we can say it is 1 Corinthians 3. How interesting that at the beginning of 1 Corinthians 3, Paul uses some of the same expressions found here. He starts out 1 Corinthians 3 this way: 'Brothers, I could not address you as spiritual but as worldly—mere infants in Christ. I gave you milk, not solid food, for you were not yet ready for it. Indeed, you are still not ready.'

Then Paul explains the problems, and ends up referring to the judgment seat of Christ. It makes me think that Paul could have written Hebrews because, in the same vein, the author writes about the milk and the meat, as we will see more of in the verses following, then goes on to talk about burning in the end for worthless products (Heb. 6:8). It is the same thing as being tried by fire in 1 Corinthians 3:13-15. I could not help but see the parallels. It is an argument for the Pauline authorship of Hebrews.

They ought to be teachers

As I mentioned earlier, the writer knew his readers. For one thing he knows how long they have been saved. He has taken into account the considerable period of time which has elapsed since their conversion. A. W. Pink speculated that some of these readers may have been called during the days of Christ's public ministry. Probably some were among the 3,000 that were converted on the day of Pentecost. If the epistle was written in or shortly after 60 A.D., as I believe, we are talking about people who had been converted for thirty years or more.

Now, to be fair, though the writer blames them for his inability to expound Melchizedek straightaway, there is an implicit admission that he is dealing with a most difficult subject. The Greek word occurs only here in the New Testament and it literally means 'things hard to interpret' or 'things difficult to understand'. If he had only stopped there! But he does not, he goes on to say, 'because you are slow to learn'. So the writer is implying that the subject of Melchizedek need not be difficult if they were in a better spiritual state.

This state undoubtedly is rooted in their spiritual aptitude, for the inability to return to repentance (meaning 'change of mind' as we will see in chapter 6) is the consequence of letting this sluggish state continue. Jesus said that if we do not bring forth fruit, we will be cut down and thrown into the fire (John 15:6). The writer has to say this to them: 'If this sluggish state of mind that you are in is not dealt with fairly soon, you ought to know you will reach the place where it will be impossible to be renewed to repentance.' It is a very serious thing for that to happen.

'Slow to learn' was the common Greek ethical term for a sluggish intelligence. (It may also have meant 'laziness'.) We are familiar with the expression, 'IQ', intelligence quotient; what we are talking about is SQ—spiritual quotient. For there is a spiritual intelligence and that is what the writer is on to. He is not talking about whether his readers are clever. You can be a good pianist and get good grades; you might have an ability to do maths; you may be a medical student and pass your exams, and get a First; that is intelligence.

But I am not referring to such. I am describing a spiritual intelligence that is traceable to one thing: obedience to Jesus Christ. The New International Version translates the Greek words *nothroi* (dull) and *akoais* (hearing) as 'slow to learn'. The Authorised Version translation 'dull of hearing' is exactly right. The writer is not talking about a natural inability to learn but a spiritual inability to *hear God's voice*. Hence the warning, 'Today, if you hear his voice' (Hebrews 3:7).

It does not come through book learning; it comes through walking in the light—honouring God, obeying him, taking his word seriously—to the extent that we will be driven to our knees to pray, and to have a heart after God. But I think so many Christians today are satisfied that they are saved, and that is all. And I suspect that many people (I do not know this, I am tempted not even to finish the sentence, but I will say it because I think it), many converted people today will suffer loss and be saved by fire at the judgment seat of Christ. The apostle Paul could not bear the thought of being like that. I hope that is the way you too look at it.

I do not know that I would push this idea too far, but perhaps this will be easily grasped: there are some that have the *gift* (office) *of teaching* and there are some that have the *grace of teaching*. 'You ought to be teachers, you need someone to teach you', refers not to the office of teaching but the grace to teach. Let me explain what I mean. For example, in Ephesians 4:11 Paul says, 'God gave some to be apostles, some to be prophets, some to be evangelists, and some to be pastors and teachers.' The same is also written in 1 Corinthians 12:28, 'And in the church God has appointed first of all apostles, second prophets, third teachers...'. That is a gift or office. I have that. I ought to be a teacher. These Hebrew Christians, however, were *not* being rebuked for not being this.

But there is another kind. For example, in Titus 2:3-15, Paul says:

Likewise, *teach* the older women to be reverent in the way they live, not to be slanderers or addicted to much wine, but to *teach* what is good. Then they can train the younger women to love their husbands and children, to be self-controlled and pure, to be busy at home, to be kind, and to be subject to their husbands, so that no-one will malign the word of God.

Similarly, encourage the young men to be self-controlled. In everything set them an example by doing what is good. In your *teaching* show integrity, seriousness and soundness of speech that cannot be condemned, so that those who oppose you may be ashamed because they have nothing bad to say about us.

Teach slaves to be subject to their masters in everything, to try to please them, not to talk back to them, and not to steal from them, but to show that they can be fully trusted, so that in every way they will make the *teaching* about God our Saviour attractive.

For the grace of God that brings salvation has appeared to all men. It *teaches* us to say 'No' to ungodliness and worldly passions, and to live self-controlled, upright and godly lives in this present age, while we wait for the blessed hope — the glorious appearing of our great God and Saviour, Jesus Christ, who gave himself for us to redeem us from all wickedness and to purify for himself a people that are his very own, eager to do what is good.

These, then, are the things you should *teach*. Encourage and rebuke with all authority. Do not let anyone despise you.

That I would call a 'grace' of teaching, even though Titus undoubtedly had the 'gift' of teaching. But it is not referring to the office of teaching. I can give you another example of the same from Acts 18:26, where Apollos, having spoken boldly in the synagogue, had the way of God explained to him more perfectly by Aquila and Priscilla: they had the 'grace' of teaching.

Can you see that this is what our writer is on to: that these people that he is addressing ought to be able to do that? It is this second kind of teaching—not the gift, not the office of being a teacher, but this ability, this grace, this strength, this spiritual intelligence, that is what the writer has in mind.

Many people are going to seminary today trying to learn theology. It is pitiful what is taught in most seminaries today, and I suppose the worst country of all is Germany. I think it is almost unheard of in Germany for those who teach in university or seminary to take the Bible seriously as the word of God. Ever since Rudolf Bultmann came up with the idea of 'demythologising' (and that phrase has caught on, certainly the idea, and swept right over Europe and throughout the world), there is an assumption in most theological schools today that the Bible is mostly myth and we need to demythologise it and get back some meaning. For example, we are not to take seriously that Christ really walked on the water; instead just demythologise and say that through Jesus we can conquer problems or difficulties.

Now when the writer says that they 'ought' to be teachers (here is where the Greek language helps us to see what the translations do not convey), it is the strongest word possible. When it is translated *ought*, we are not to think about the subjunctive mood which is translated that one 'should' do this. Rather, it is a separate word meaning to be 'indebted to', to 'be bound'. His point is that by this time they are bound to be teachers. So it is a serious position to be in when one's potential teachers are at an immature stage. In other words, their time had come and they were found wanting. It is possible for the mind to stand still when dealing with the utterances of God. If the dark things do not become plain, then the plain things will become dark.

It is quite extraordinary that one so gloriously saved can let the years go by and not grow in grace. Remember that from those to whom much is given, much shall be required. In the parable of the Pounds or Talents in Matthew 25:14-30, each was given a certain amount, call it a talent, although it really meant money in those days. Today we say we are not very 'talented' and in a way that is an unfortunate translation because Jesus is not describing an ability to play the piano, but talking about a spiritual aptitude. But because it is a parable, Jesus gave a material example to be spiritually applied. In a word: we are to multiply spiritually.

This multiplication can be understood in at least two ways. Firstly, the multiplying of our faith so that it becomes the fruits of the Spirit (the main and most important thing). Secondly, it may refer to our reaching others with the gospel and seeing them converted.

There were, therefore, those who multiplied, who added to their faith, goodness; and to goodness, knowledge; and to knowledge, self-control; and to self-control, perseverance; and to perseverance, godliness, etc. And they were sharp and able and, very possibly, some became soul-winners. Did you realise that the teaching aspect can also include the ability to lead a person to Jesus Christ? And the case can be made that the writer to the Hebrews is burdened by the fact that his readers ought to have been multiplying all this time. I wonder myself how many of my readers who have been Christians for many years, have never led a soul to Jesus Christ? And probably never will if it has not happened by now. Unless one is severely jolted and convicted.

It is likely that those who are described in Hebrews 6:4-6 could previously have been described like those in this verse, for Hebrews 5:11-12 portrays what I could call a pre-malignant state. Hebrews 5:11-12 does not point to an irreversible, inoperable malignancy. It merely shows warning signs. When a person who has been saved for a while is not really developing into genuine maturity, there is cause for alarm. Those described in Hebrews 6:4-6 were once as those described as being 'dull of hearing' and who 'ought to be teachers'. For, when it comes to your spiritual sense, if you do not use it, you lose it; if you do not walk in the light, you go backwards. So they were back to square one, they had actually lost a measure of hearing. How did this happen? Through neglect. That is why in chapter 2:3 he wrote, 'How shall we escape if we ignore such a great salvation?' He did not say *reject*, he said *ignore* so great salvation.

This is the explanation of the person who eventually

overthrows his evangelical heritage. Let me explain what I mean. Did you ever meet somebody who at one time was an evangelical, who believed the simple gospel that Jesus died on the cross for his or her sins, and trusted in him for salvation, but right now cannot be taught the same gospel because he or she does not really believe it? They believed it at one time, and were saved.

I think I had a professor like this, on the other side of the Atlantic, who, I happen to know, for years after he was converted was a glorious Christian. Then he got involved with Bultmann, but before that took seriously the theology of Karl Barth and Paul Tillich. And do you know, he no longer believes that you are saved just by trusting in the death of Jesus Christ on the cross. I am not this man's judge and I am not claiming to know what his state is. But I am personally convinced he had a true conversion. His love for the Bible, the hours and hours he spent memorising Scripture, his love for truth convinces me this man was not counterfeit. I believe he is with the Lord today. But he reached a stage in his older years that he was not able to change his mind in a truly God-wise direction. He was a teacher (a professor) but unteachable.

What happens is that a person like that no longer believes even the first principles, and this is a sad thing. Although that is a more extreme case, it partly explains how it can happen. So the way to know that you are walking in the light, partly, is that you are brought back to the death of Jesus all the time. The person of Jesus thus remains real: his resurrection, his death on the cross. Once a person departs from that and tries to get into other kinds of learning, he somehow never gets back to the ABCs.

The main point is that the writer blames them for their inability to teach others truth. Some people might blame themselves. I think a lot of teachers, myself included, if our congregations are not benefiting from what we teach, would react by blaming ourselves: I am just not being clear enough, I will try it again. The writer is not as insecure as that. He just blames them. He says that the problem is that they have become so dull of hearing; they cannot handle the deep things of God, owing to a serious spiritual defect in themselves. So the way he puts it is this: you ought to be teachers; in other words, by this time you ought to be in a position to help other people.

There comes a time when you must begin to help others. I know some Christians who after years and years and years are still needing the same old kind of help. It has not entered their minds to help anybody else. They figure if they once get sorted out *then* they will be on their way to help somebody else. They say, 'I'm getting there, I'm almost ready, but I have got to get this problem solved.' Yet years later they are still in much the same condition! Often the best way to solve your problem is to get your eyes completely off yourself and start helping somebody else. Your own problems begin to diminish!

The person who cannot handle solid food has to have milk. How are you going to reach a person in that condition?

My own view would be that the writer hoped that his own letter would change their outlook. In other words, 'internal chastening', that is, when God's word arrests you and you wake up. God just operates. But then there is the 'external chastening', Plan B, when God has to work through circumstances to bring you low. It can be through loss; it can be through disappointment; it can be through health, whatever. It has to be external because we do not take in the warning, we do not take the hint, and God has to do something else. But worst of all is 'terminal chastening', what takes place on the day of Christ. But it is also being stone deaf; the inability to hear God and be renewed again to repentance. 'Terminal chastening' is an apt phrase for those described in Hebrews 6:4-6.

The word of God

What is it that they would have to be taught? The phrase used is 'the elementary truths of God's word'. The literal translation is 'the beginning of the elementary things', and this is why many modern translations just call it the ABCs. What the writer is saying to these Hebrew Christians is that they need the ABCs.

The big question is, What are the ABCs?

The medieval commentators, from the twelfth century up to Calvin's time, regarded the ABCs as the Apostles' Creed. But I really believe, and this is what most commentators are agreed on, that the first principles of the oracles of God are nothing more than what we have in chapter 6:1-2. There are six listed: repentance, faith, baptism, laying on of hands, resurrection of the dead, eternal judgment. That is what the writer calls ABCs.

The phrase 'God's word' (NIV) or 'oracles of God' (AV) literally means 'principles'. Stephen used the word in Acts 7:38, 'He [Moses] was in the assembly in the desert, with the angel who spoke to him on Mount Sinai, with our fathers; and he received *living words* to pass on to us.' It is found in Romans 3:2, after Paul raised the question, What advantage, then, is there in being a Jew, or what value is there in circumcision? He says, 'Much in every way! First of all, they have been entrusted with the *very words* of God.' Now in these two places, this is the word which is specifically used to describe the Old Testament. Stephen referring to Sinai; Paul to the fact simply that the word of God was given to the Jews. But then in 1 Peter 4:11, Peter says, 'If anyone speaks [and he is referring now to the minister], he should do it as one speaking the *very words* of God.'

Peter's point is that the minister of the gospel should speak believing that what he says is the very word of God, as much as what was given to Moses at Sinai, what was given to the Jews. So it is something that would search any preacher's heart. It is an awesome thing to realise that we are called upon to preach, speaking as the words of God.

What the writer says is, You instead need to be taught the ABCs of the word of God. The implication then is that there are two parts of this: (1) The ABCs, which would be what the writer calls 'milk'; (2) the other would be what Paul would call the 'deep things' of God, or meat (the Greek word means 'solid food').

What a pity, then, that these Hebrew Christians were right back to square one, needing milk not solid food. It is almost a sarcastic statement. He says 'that is where you are.' It is like a person who physically is in such a bad shape that all he can take is milk, and he cannot have anything else to eat. It is a blatant rebuke. If milk is the only diet suited to a certain physical condition, it shows that one is in a serious state; but spiritually the writer means that one is in an immature but potentially dangerous state. It suggests an *arrested development*.

This is something that can happen to people emotionally, and it can happen to them spiritually. What does this mean? Well, take emotionally. You have seen people who appear to be old, but emotionally they are not mature. Why is that? Well they have got a physical age of say, 30, 40, 50, but an emotional age that might be 4 or 8 or 12 or 15. No matter how long a person lives they are not really getting any older emotionally. Now when a person, let's say, is an 18 year old but has an emotional age of 15, probably he will get away with it, no one thinks too much about it. They say the person is just a little immature, and they think he will be better by the time he is 21. Yet at the age of 40, he is still only 15. There are various explanations why this can take place at a psychological level and I do not need to go into that. I think most would be agreed that this is simply a fact of human nature.

But what the writer here is doing is using the term that suggests this very concept, not psychologically but spiritually. So if a person has an arrested development spiritually, then no matter how many more years he lives, he does not automatically get any better. Here is the person who has been converted and he or she is going fine for six months, or two years, or five years, or ten years, but then something happens. Maybe disappointment in their life. Maybe the loss of their job. And so the person is tried. But if he or she does not dignify the trial, if they do not learn to forgive, if they do not grow in grace and walk in the light, something backfires internally; they might continue going to church, but there is an arrested development, and they never move on.

Now that is the principle that the writer is discussing. He is very worried about them, and yet he is not worried. Although he first warns them, at the end he says, 'we are confident of better things in your case' (6:9). It is similar to what Paul had to say to the Corinthians: 'I could not address you as spiritual but as worldly—mere infants in Christ. I gave you milk, not solid food, for you were not yet ready for it. Indeed, you are still not ready.' Do you know what this tells me? In a way it is encouraging, for you always get a little bit of encouragement if you know that others have had the same problem. It just shows how frequently this has been repeated. We know that Paul wrote to the Corinthians regarding this problem; somebody wrote to the Hebrews saying exactly the same thing. It seems to be a pattern.

Every one who lives on milk is *out of his depth* when it comes to the word of righteousness. The one whose diet is milk would be out of his depth with teachings such as Melchizedek being a figure of the priestly work of Christ. Because they have become so slothful, they actually need the ABCs. The question is, why would the writer even *bother* with people like this? What did the writer see in them that would devote this whole epistle to them?

I have thought about this in connection with myself, because I am absolutely sure that I have been like them, yet God is patient with me. I think of Jonah—why did God send the fish to swallow up Jonah? But he did, and I know what it is to be a Jonah. People used to ask me why I chose Jonah to preach my first sermons at Westminster Chapel. The answer is I am Jonah. God is so patient with me. I say to God, 'Why have you given me such attention as you have?'

These people were out of their depth because the one who uses milk is unacquainted with the word of righteousness, for he is a baby. This expression 'word of righteousness'—I do not think there is any need to go into any great detail here.

We could write a whole book in saying that it might refer to justification by faith—and some have thought that is what it meant. Others, Calvin for example, and I would tend to agree with him here, think that it is a broader expression, that it just means the ability to discern, because the writer goes on to say in verse 14, (we will deal with it in the next chapter), 'Solid food is for the mature, who by constant use have trained themselves to distinguish good from evil.' So being skilful in the word of righteousness probably does not mean justification by faith, but rather, being able to discern between good and evil.

And yet, if we find ourselves described in Hebrews 5:11-12, it is not the end! It certainly does not mean we will end up like those described in Hebrews 6:4-6. There was hope for these Hebrew Christians — 'we are confident of better things in your case'—and there is hope for each of us who hear God speaking in these lines.

2

Growing Pains

Anyone who lives on milk, being still an infant, is not acquainted with the teaching about righteousness. But solid food is for the mature, who by constant use have trained themselves to distinguish good from evil (Hebrews 5:13-14).

What needs to be driven home is something that I think we tend to take not too seriously, that is, the importance of growing in grace. 'But grow in the grace and knowledge of our Lord and Saviour Jesus Christ' (2 Pet. 3:18). Growth in grace is not an option, we ought to grow in grace. The Bible teaches that there are serious consequences for not doing so. And that is precisely what we are looking at in this book.

The writer says, in verses 13 and 14, that remaining a child after many years is not on. As I have already said in the previous chapter, we have reason to believe that we are thinking about Christians who had been converted for up to thirty years. By now they ought to be teachers, but the pity is that they need the ABCs.

What happens to believers who do not grow? I can tell you what happens. They degenerate to what Paul calls 'worldly', 'carnal' in the AV (1 Cor. 3). If they do not eventually grow and develop, you can mark down two absolutely certain consequences. First, they will fall away so as to make entering God's rest an utter impossibility; and secondly, at the judgment seat of Christ they will be saved, 'but only as one escaping through the flames' (1 Cor. 3:15).

Regarding this childishness, Calvin commented that there is a two-fold childishness. First, there is a type of person who *never matures*, and just develops a habit of carelessness. This is why James wrote, 'Anyone who chooses to be a friend of the world becomes an enemy of God' (Jas. 4:4). But there is also a

childishness of *sense*, that is, of the ability to grasp the truth, and
James said of that person that the 'double-minded man is
unstable in all he does' (1:8). When we talk about childishness
then, two things stand out. One is that a child is careless, the
other that the child is ignorant. Both aspects, the writer says,
mark these Hebrew Christians.

Solid food is for the mature
The NIV rendering 'solid food' is translated 'strong meat' in the
Authorised Version. What is meant here is this: the writer refers
to a manner of knowing the truth. Or you could say, he refers to
doctrine that cannot be perceived except in the realm of the
Spirit. This kind of teaching is what Paul called being spiritually
discerning, as we read in 1 Corinthians 2:14: 'The man without
the Spirit does not accept the things that come from the Spirit of
God, for they are foolishness to him, and he cannot understand
them because they are spiritually discerned.'

The kind of teaching that the writer means, when he writes
'strong meat is for the mature', is a teaching that cannot simply
be meted out by a catechism. It cannot be formulated by a creed.
It is something beyond the natural level. Now there is a place for
the catechism—I once wrote a catechism, I do not think it was
a very good one. I shared it with different people who said it was
all right, but I did not try to push it too hard. But I believe in the
value of the catechism, and some day I would like to write a
systematic theology. I am not against doctrine, I am not against
systematising truth. I think it is crucial. It is what Paul calls
rightly dividing the word of truth.

But, understanding doctrine, though you put it systematically,
is not what the writer means here. Whenever we talk about
formulating doctrine, we really are talking about something that
can be understood to some degree even at the natural level.

There are a lot of people who think, because they are
beginning to understand some great truths, that they are into the
deep things of God. An example is the doctrine of election—I
mean, that is pretty heavy. Since it is profound, some find it hard

to grasp, and many rebel against it. But if they *do* have the breakthrough and understand it, they think that they have made a giant step and are somehow into the deep things of God. Do you not realise that even election is part of the ABCs?

Another example is Melchizedek. He was someone that these Hebrew Christians would have never thought of. But the writer says they should have, if they were where they ought to be. They would have read Psalm 110 that says, 'You are a priest for ever, in the order of Melchizedek' and they would understand its significance. That is the kind of teaching that is spiritually discerned. It is doctrine, but it is not the kind of teaching that can be quickly pigeon-holed. The writer's point is that he is not simply talking about doctrine that can be put into propositions. He is talking about being plugged into a divine network so that you can read the Old Testament with understanding, and, I think he would agree, read the New Testament with understanding too. They did not have the New Testament, for it was still being written. What did the earliest Christians do? What was their basis of doctrine? The early church had to go to the Old Testament, and it was important for them to be able to read it with understanding, but the Hebrews were not doing that. It had become vague to them. So, what *can* be put into a system, the writer would call the ABCs.

Now had these people been where they ought to have been, they could have accepted all that he is going to say about Melchizedek, for they would have been ready for it. As soon as they heard it, they would say, 'Ah, I was thinking the same thing.' Say a person is in school. If he or she is doing the homework and is up to date on what has been taught, they will be so ready for the next lecture that they will say they were wondering if it would be that way.

The ministry of the Spirit

Now, the Christian faith is not merely head knowledge. This is why we have the Holy Spirit who teaches us in such a way that we do not remain helpless and ignorant. What can be more basic than our need for the Holy Spirit to guide us? Many have let book-learning, systematic theology, creed, doctrine replace the Holy Spirit. And for this reason, many Christians today, I fear, have very little experience of the Spirit of God showing them things, guiding them in the truth, seeing things are real and definite, and right from God. So many of us are in a mould that it does not even enter our minds to break out of, we are just in a closed circuit, and the Spirit never shows us anything.

The reason that the Spirit will not show us anything is that he is grieved. One way we grieve the Spirit is by *bitterness*. This is the dimension that I have been trying to put forward ever since I came to Westminster Chapel: this matter of love. I once wrote an article for the Westminster Record on the subject, 'Can Calvinism and Arminianism be married?' I believe the answer is, yes. If so it means that both are going to have to concede certain things and I will mention what some of them are. The Arminians are going to have to agree the doctrine of election is true, and once a person is saved, he is always saved. The Calvinists likewise need to see that what John Wesley taught about love was right, but many Calvinists have dismissed it, because it was Arminian. Whenever I look for a hymn on love (and interestingly enough, a good hymn on the intercessory work of Christ), I have to go to Charles Wesley. There are exceptions, but most of the great hymns on the intercessory work of Christ and walking in love are by Charles Wesley.

My point is, when we do not forgive one another and we let any kind of bitterness creep in, the Spirit is grieved and it causes a short circuit. Nothing happens, nothing connects, and we do not grow. I believe this with all my heart. So many have not taken seriously this matter of walking in love and, in consequence of that, have not been able to walk in the light. It does not seem to bother them a bit, if they judge another person, if they hold a grudge, if they cannot speak to certain people in the same congregation. Look, this is wrong! The Spirit is grieved. Do you know what else that means? It means that they do not grow, although they come to church week after week, month after month, and year after year. This is what had happened to some of these Hebrew Christians.

We need to learn that the Christian faith is not like maths or physics, because what we need is not intellectual acumen, but the Spirit to show us things. This is why you can meet somebody who has not been to Oxford or Cambridge or even into a Sixth Form or done 'O' levels or GCSEs, but who can have the profoundest knowledge of God. I have run into people who could barely write their names, but at whose feet I would sit and let them explain to me things about the Bible. How do you explain that? Simply, there are those who refuse to let the Spirit be grieved in their life.

What can we do to get the breakthrough?

To achieve the breakthrough requires fulfilling three simple conditions.

First, *dignify the trial*. By dignifying the trial, I mean that when anything comes our way that does not set well with us at first, we might be rocked, we may be jolted. It may be severe but we respond positively to it, rather than murmur. Rather, we say, 'Lord, you have given me a severe trial, but this is one trial (or to use the synonym, test,) that I want to pass. Help me to pass it, by not complaining, by waiting, and not try to get it over with prematurely.' Let it run its full course, as James said, 'Consider it pure joy,... perseverance must finish its work' (1:2, 4). Just wait, because it will end, and when it ends, we can have the joy of knowing that we waited. And I make you a promise: God is going to be real to us in a way we never thought possible, and we will start understanding the Bible in a new way.

Secondly, *total forgiveness*: that means we release that person who knows how we feel about them and is afraid to be around us. They are afraid to look at us because they know what we think—but we must let them know that we love them. Incidentally, it does not mean we go up to them and say, 'Well, I forgive you for what you have done'—that is just getting at them again. That is punishment, not forgiveness. Forgiveness is when they can really feel that there is nothing there. Now that may take some doing and you may say you cannot do that. But then you will never know what we are on to here in Hebrews 5. You have got to do it, and when you give to that other person the conviction that he or she is totally, utterly, and absolutely forgiven, the result will be a warmth, and a peace, and a joy in your heart that you never knew before.

Thirdly, *the willingness to become nothing*. That means that we will let that person walk all over us. We will be willing to be misunderstood. This is the theme I develop in another book, *Meekness and Majesty*.[1]

I will guarantee this, if ever I was safe in offering a guarantee in my whole life, that if we put those three principles into operation, we will begin to know what the writer means by 'strong meat'. You will realise that he is not talking about systematising truth, he is talking about that which is not obvious at the natural level. It is a breakthrough in understanding, so that the clear mind perceives what is there.

Spiritual maturity

'Mature' means full age. It is the Greek word that means 'complete'. Incidentally, Calvin describes this stage as middle-age; the picture of a person moving spiritually from infancy through teen years and becoming middle aged—a mature person spiritually. What is implicit here is that one will not get to this stage the first day after conversion. If you were saved a week ago, it is not likely that you are going to be held accountable for what those who have been Christians for years are accountable. The person who is newly converted needs milk (1 Pet. 2:2). By that is meant the ABCs, it means learning the doctrines, it means learning theology. The new Christian needs to do this to grow.

But there comes a time when one penetrates a dimension; it is *the realm of the Spirit*, when God is real, and the Bible is alive. After all, do we believe in the priesthood of all believers or not?

---

1. *Meekness and Majesty* is published by Christian Focus Publications.

Do you need a pastor or another Christian to tell you whether something is right? If you do, where are you different from the person who has to have his minister or priest to tell him what is true and what is not true? We must believe in the priesthood of the *believer*, and you do not have to be a Reverend or Doctor for God to show you things: 'No eye has seen, no ear has heard, no mind has conceived what God has prepared for those who love him—but God has revealed it to us by his Spirit' (1 Cor. 2:9-10). That means that every single believer is equally qualified, and the fact that one is a minister or has been to seminary does not necessarily give one a head start. The writer is not talking about a quantity of knowledge, but about a way of knowing.

So the problem was that there were those who were on milk, because that is all they could take. I think that there are far too many like that, all they want is to have their ears tickled. They want to hear certain things, and fancy that they are listening to the deep things of God, when really it just pleases them, and it is not spiritual. It is something that is at the natural level and they do not realise it.

3

Maturity

Therefore let us leave the elementary teachings about Christ and go on to maturity (Hebrews 6:1a).

The sixth chapter of Hebrews begins with the word 'therefore'. There are many great chapters in the Bible that have this word at the beginning: Romans 5:1—'Therefore, since we have been justified through faith, we have peace with God through our Lord Jesus Christ'; Romans 8:1—'Therefore, there is now no condemnation for those who are in Christ Jesus'; Romans 12:1—'Therefore, I urge you, brothers, in view of God's mercy...'.

Any time we see the word, 'therefore', we need to see why it is there, so we must back up several verses. Although this is always important, it is especially so with this section of Hebrews because one of the difficulties that many are hampered with in their understanding of Hebrews 6 is they forget the context, which begins in Hebrews 5:12. (Often chapter divisions can unintentionally militate against a good understanding of a passage.) Every text has a context. Campbell Morgan used to say, 'A text without a context is a pretext'. We must also remember that the general context of Hebrews 6 is that these dull Christians are in danger of forfeiting their opportunity to enter God's rest (Heb. 4:1). And yet though they are in danger, the writer ends up saying, 'Even though we speak like this, dear friends, we are confident of better things in your case—things that accompany salvation' (Heb. 6:9).

I want to show you how certain words used in verse 1 relate to the context. If you look back at Hebrews 5:12, it reads, 'Though by this time you ought to be teachers, you need someone to teach you the *elementary truths* of God's word all over again.' And in verse 14, the writer talks about those who are 'mature'. These expressions that come in Hebrews 6:1, all go back to the context. So, the 'elementary teachings' refers back to the 'elementary truths' of 5:12, and 'maturity' to 'the mature' of 5:14. If you read this passage in the Authorized Version you will find that verse 1 says 'let us go on unto perfection'. We need to understand that the word 'perfection' means 'full growth' or 'maturity', as the newer versions have it.

Now maturity or 'full growth' is precisely what these Hebrew Christians did not have, despite the fact that some of them probably had been converted for thirty years. We tend to feel that maturity is a good thing if we have it but do not worry too much if we do not. It is as though maturity is an optional thing, which we can take or leave. But what we are going to see more and more is that the one who is never weaned from the diet of milk will in the end be unable to have anything but milk. As I pointed out in the previous chapter, solid food is *not a reference to certain theological propositions, but the nourishment by which our capacity to understand is enlarged.*

I want to stress the word *habit* here. That is an important thing to realise and this needs to be driven home. For when the writer says in verse 14, 'Solid food is for the mature, who by *constant use* have trained themselves...', it is a Greek word that literally means, habit. And so the NIV translates it 'constant use'. The dictionary definition of habit is 'aptitude acquired by practice'.

What is habit?

Habit is when you do not have to think twice about anything. You just do things, you do not realise you are doing them. When you are driving, you see a green light but it turns yellow, then red. You naturally slow down and stop. Rain comes down, you put up your umbrella. You would not even be aware of it. Now what the writer is after is that these Christians will reach a level of maturity that becomes a habit. Some Christians once in a while get really inspired and want to please the Lord. But they are conscious of it, so it is not a habit.

If we reach a level of Christian maturity that it becomes a habit, then we are not even aware of it, it is just automatic. What this means is that what would be an ordeal for a new Christian is one that a maturer believer abides with dignity. We would not be surprised if a new Christian panics when he has a sudden trial, even if up to then he was doing fine and was all aglow with the joy of the Lord. But what about the mature Christian? Well, he or she is like Job, when his wife came to him and said, 'Why do you not curse God and die?' And Job said, 'You speak like a foolish woman.' Why did Job say that? Habit. It did not enter his mind to complain to God. So as a consequence of developing this habit, we gain what we could call a sixth sense, but a spiritual one.

I am amazed at some of the more superficial commentaries which stress that what the writer means here is that we ought to study our Bibles, memorise scripture, etc. I really believe we should memorise scripture, read our Bibles, go to church and pray, etc., but that is not what the writer is on about at all, however important it is. He is talking about where the person by constant use has developed an unconscious ability to receive things from God. As I wrote in the previous chapter, three things lead to this condition: dignifying the trial, totally forgiving your brother or your sister or any person who has mistreated you, and becoming nothing. That has got to become a habit. If you are conscious of doing these things, for example, you are forgiving your brother and at the same time thinking you have really done something great, it shows it is not a habit yet. But when it is a lifestyle that you totally forgive people and you just do it, because it is a part of you—that is what he means by constant use; the result is a perception by which you are able to distinguish good and evil.

What the writer means by maturity, or 'perfection', is developing the habit so that the result is a sixth sense by which you are able to distinguish between good and evil. Or as the New English Bible puts it, 'discriminate good from evil'. So we read in Romans 12:2, 'Do not conform any longer to the pattern of this world, but be transformed by the renewing of your mind. Then you will be able to test and approve what God's will is— his good, pleasing and perfect will.' So by having the habit we are not conformed to this world, we are being renewed, there is this sixth sense, and we are able to know the good, pleasing and perfect will of God. Perfection, or maturity, is not a certain set of doctrines. What the writer means is an instrument, a mechanism in us that is tuned to the heavenly network so we can hear God's voice.

God said to Abraham, 'Take your son Isaac, your only son, and go to Mount Moriah and sacrifice him.' And do you know what? Abraham did it! He said, 'I do not know what God has got in mind, I guess he is going to raise Isaac from the dead.' At any rate he obeyed. In other words, it was a habit. It did not occur to him to do anything else but what God said, because that was a way of life with Abraham. He had acquired such a habit by that time, so when God required that difficult action from him, Abraham did not think twice. The same was true of Shadrach, Meshach and Abednego. They did not need to call a committee meeting and decide what they were going to do when the music next was played. They did not even need to look at each other. Habit. They knew where they were.

What are the outworkings of this sixth sense? I would put it this way. First, we *will* be able to smell heresy or false doctrine. Second, we will be able to spot hypocrisy, which does not mean we go around saying someone is a hypocrite, but we will have this faithful testimony within, and we will not be misled. Thirdly, we will be able to discern honesty.

An abused word

I want to look in more detail at the word 'maturity', 'full growth'. It is a scary word, when we use it in the sense of 'perfection', partly because it is a word that has been abused. What you have got, I think, are two extremes: one extreme was taught by John Wesley, where you border very perilously on a sinless perfection. Methodism was born in revival, do not ever forget that. The danger is that when the glory of God begins to subside a bit, theologians come behind and systematise what had been a valid experience in the first generation. That is how we got the perfectionist movement. It is one extreme.

The other extreme is to say that we know we are not perfect and there is no use thinking about it. We all sin and the desire to attain perfection is completely lost. When such people read a word about going on to perfection, it does not bother them. They would say, 'We know we cannot attain to it, so why bother?' That is the other extreme.

What I intend to do is to show that we need to take this word seriously for it does not mean either extreme. I believe it means two things.

The ability to digest solid food

That is the first thing. Solid food is nourishment by which the capacity of the soul is enlarged. Sooner or later, a new-born baby must go from milk to something solid, and if that does not happen there will be a deformed child. It is the same analogy here.

What do I mean then when I say solid food is nourishment by which the capacity of the soul is enlarged? The soul's enlargement will mean simple trust in God, unfeigned love of one another, and the ability to understand what God is pleased to reveal. Now by simple trust in God, I would remind you of 1 John 4:16, 'we know and rely on the love God has for us'. That verse has gripped me for years. But it involves simple trust, simply taking seriously that God really does love us. When one really believes it, it changes everything. The ability to digest solid food is the enlargement of the soul, where you become able, simply in a childlike way, to trust in God. Jesus said, 'Anyone who will not receive the kingdom of God like a little child will never enter it.' Christians need to rediscover this simple trust in God, which is the soul's enlargement.

These Hebrew Christians were caught high and dry when it became apparent that they could not handle Melchizedek. Failure to move on in terms of God's revelation was what exposed them. The lesson from that is this: nobody knows what your faith is truly like. We really do not know each other that well. I simply do not know whether another believer has a simple trust in God, a child-like faith, like George Müeller had when he prayed in a simple, believing manner for what was needed day-by-day in the orphanages in Bristol. George Müeller was quick to say that he did not have the gift of faith of 1 Corinthians 12, it was just a simple trust, the faith that every Christian ought to have. I am telling you, we are in this together, and it is not going to do us any good to pose as some great spiritual giant, because at the judgment seat of Christ we are going to find out who really walked with the Lord.

The ability to perceive

I am referring here to the ability to perceive God's will. That has to do with aptitude to receive what God wants to say. It is understanding his word, and it is knowing his direction for today. It is his word, and his will.

Understanding his word is simply being able to read the Bible and know what it means, that God speaks to you. And so, as I have said, Psalm 110:4: 'The Lord has sworn... you are a priest for ever, in the order of Melchizedek.' The writer is saying they ought to know what that verse meant. Well, they did not know, and he knew they did not.

Maturity includes seeing his will. By this I mean that you know God so well that you know what he is thinking. As I get to know some of my congregation, I can tell where they are, what they are thinking. It is the same with my wife, I do not have to tell her or ask her what she thinks, I already know. When you know God, you know his will.

Jonathan Edwards emphasised that the task of every generation is to discover in which direction the sovereign Redeemer is moving, then move in that direction. Every generation must be open. This is the thing Edwards saw, and it is the legacy he left that so many who admire him do not pick up on. He taught that

God wants to *start* from square one, every time; but the second generation, it seems, always wants to perpetuate the first without moving on.

But Edwards knew that if we are going to have the glory of God we need to start again from the beginning. Milk is what we desire if we want to go back to the good old days. Those who are not emancipated from tradition can never be convinced that this is their problem. They are still worldly, they are babes, saved thirty or forty years, still wanting to go back, go back, go back.

I think it might be helpful for some if I were to use a little acrostic, PEACE, on how to know the will of God. None of us wants to be deceived when we are open. How may we know we are not being deceived?

First, is it *Providential*? In other words, if you are praying whether to do this or that, does it fall in place, do you have to nudge the arm of providence, or does it just happen? If somebody comes up to me and says, 'I feel led to preach at Westminster Chapel', I will reply, 'Well, if the Holy Spirit is really leading you, I will feel led to invite you.' So, is it providential?

Second: *Enemy*. Always put this in the computer when you are wanting to know the will of God: what will the devil think? Would it please the devil or displease him? You would be surprised how quickly you can know the will of God, when you just put that in the computer. Do the opposite of what the devil would want.

Third, *Authority*. What does the Bible say? Is it biblical, in other words. The Holy Spirit will never lead us to embrace what is contrary to Holy Scripture.

Fourth, *Confidence*. What does this do for your own confidence? your own assurance? sense of wellbeing? Because whenever you are in the will of God, it will increase your sense of confidence. It always does that. When you are lacking in confidence, there is something wrong. If what you are about to do diminishes your confidence, there is something wrong.

Fifthly, *Ease*. Does this decision give you a feeling of ease? 'To thine own self be true', as Shakespeare put it.

So PEACE. That is how to know the will of God. Now this acrostic can be a kind of guide, and yet, if you develop the godly habit, you will not necessarily need this. I do not say it will not be helpful, but that it will simply confirm what you have found to be true anyway.

When the writer says, let us 'go on to maturity', he is not merely asking that we finally deal with this doctrine or that doctrine. He is talking about being able to grasp something beyond the ABCs. So, he says, let us leave the elementary teaching.

There are those who still want to feast on things that they should have mastered in the first eighteen months of their Christian life, for this is all they still want. I used to be invited to preach in a particular church in South Florida. It was a Dutch Calvinist church, and do you know, every Sunday night, without fail (by rule, they did not have any choice), they taught the Heidelberg Catechism. These old saints had been having it for forty years, and they think that is the deep things of God. People have misunderstood what is meant by meat. They think that because they are getting some heavy doctrine that it is meat. That is not at all what the writer means. Meat is nourishment, by which your capacity to grasp is enlarged. If you keep just getting ABCs all the time, you are not expanding.

How would you feel if you went to your son or daughter's sixth form and you asked permission to sit in on a class and the teacher came in and said, All right, everyone, here we go together: ABCDEFG... Or you go to Oxford University to hear a sophisticated lecture and the professor comes out and says: ABCDEFGHIJK... You would say, What is going on here? Yet there are long-standing Christians, who are still churning out the same old thing and have not learned anything in years. That is what the writer is on about: Christians who want the same old thing over and over again, who are not even thinking of any kind of growth. The truth is they have had an arrested development. And that is the danger, that doctrine becomes an end, rather than a means.

And so the writer says, 'Let us cease' (this is the way Calvin translated the verse) to speak of the elementary teachings about Christ. The writer introduces then a twofold elaboration or exhortation. He says, 'Let us leave and let us go on.' What is it we leave? We leave the ABCs. What is it we go on to? We go on to this habit by which we are able to grasp things. Now, note this principle, those who never get beyond the beginnings, never mature at all. And this is why not entering God's rest and falling away are the same thing.

The AV says, 'Let us go on'; the NIV just says, 'Go on'; the Phillips translation: 'Go forward'; the Revised Version: 'Let us press on'. But Bishop Westcott makes an interesting observation and I am grateful for this: he points out that the Greek literally means, 'Let us be borne on'. Do you know that the word, used here where it says, Let us go on, is the same Greek word used in 2 Peter 1:21 when the writer says that holy men spoke as they were 'borne along' or 'carried along' by the Spirit. The way the Bible was written, was that they were borne along by the Spirit. All we need do is open ourselves to God and he will bear us up.

As Philip Edgecumbe Hughes puts it, 'It is not a matter for learners being carried by their instructor, but rather both instructor and learner being carried along by God. It is the energy of the Holy Spirit.' It is a word that simultaneously means 'we go on' and yet we go on as we are borne along. It is an encouragement to realise that it is not entirely up to us at all. We have got to fight, yes, for it is the fight of faith; we have got to struggle, and the writer warns of the danger of coming short. Yet to those who simply say, 'God, I want to do what you want me to do,' and just open their hearts to him, he will take such seriously. John says his commandments are not grievous, are not burdensome. We are carried along and begin to grow.

Maturity is the aptitude to receive whatever God wants to say. Jesus had to say to his disciples, 'I have many things to say to you but you cannot bear them now.' Maturity is being able to bear them, so that we are where God wants us to be; and when he speaks to us we hear, we listen.

4

The Foundation In General

Therefore let us leave the elementary teachings about Christ and go on to maturity, not laying again the foundation of repentance from acts that lead to death, and of faith in God (Hebrews 6:1).

More than one commentator has made the point, that if you would put a bracket, a parenthesis, right after 'maturity', just before the word 'not', and go all the way down to the end of verse 2, and end the parenthesis after 'judgment', you will understand the thinking of the writer. So we could be forgiven for reading it like this: 'Therefore let us leave the elementary teachings about Christ and go on to maturity, and God permitting, we will do so.' That does no harm to the meaning, it only clarifies it, and no matter what your view is of the verses to follow, this is certainly a valid way to look at these verses. What we have in parentheses is: 'not laying again the foundation of repentance from acts that lead to death, and of faith in God, instructions about baptisms, the laying on of hands, the resurrection of the dead, and eternal judgment.'

Those who never get beyond the beginnings, never mature at all. This is why not entering God's rest is the same thing as what the writer will call 'falling away' in the verses coming up. So either way, coming short of entering into God's rest, or having been enlightened, having tasted of the good word of God and the powers of the world to come, to come so far and then fall away—it is exactly the same thing. The writer in saying, 'Let us leave' wants the Hebrew believers to progress from those ABCs. His hope for these Hebrew Christians, as was Paul's hope for the Corinthians, is that they would go on. 'You are still worldly,' said Paul, in his letter to Corinth. What does the writer say to his hearers? 'You are still babies, children.' It is the same principle exactly.

In Hebrews 4:1, we have the exhortation: 'Therefore, since the promise of entering his rest still stands, let us be careful that none of you be found to have fallen short of it.' They had been given saving faith and seen that Jesus died on the cross for their sins, and yet because they became enamoured with this or that (as in the case of those Christians in Corinth, where some followed Apollos, some followed Cephas, and they were divided among themselves), if they were to die as they were, they would be saved only as by fire. But Paul knew there was a better way for them, and this is why there are exhortations in Corinthians that are not unlike those in Hebrews.

I think it is something that is often overlooked. The big mistake that so many have made with regard to the book of Hebrews is that they think that it is a different kind of book because it was written to Jews. But this book is just like all the other books in the New Testament. The fact that it is called 'Hebrews' does not change the interpretation, because in God's scheme we are all one, and there is not a different set of doctrine for Jews, and another set for Gentiles.

The writer's concern is for those who never get beyond the beginnings, that is, they never mature. Coming up to the place where they might have entered into God's rest, something happens, they just do not enter in. And if they never *do*, they reach the place, alas, where they never *can*. That is what the writer was worried about. He feared that they had reached the place where they never could enter, and I hope that that would not be the case with any one reading this book. Falling away, then, is failure to go on to maturity.

This failure has a certain consequence. It is that one cannot be renewed to repentance. It means that such a person never can enter into God's rest. There is a stage that one reaches so that from then on, entering God's rest is not even an option; once that stage has been reached then it is impossible to be renewed again to repentance. A person like that will be saved, but he will be saved as by fire, at the judgment seat of Christ.

A modern situation

The first phrase in the parenthesis is 'Not laying again the foundation of repentance from acts that lead to death'. A. W. Pink points out that laying the foundation *again* was precisely what these Hebrew Christians were sorely tempted to do. They wanted to *keep* their diet of milk. Mothers know what it is like when their child does not want anything but milk, and they have to wean the child. Here were the Hebrew Christians, wanting to go back, wanting to lay the foundation again. They looked for every reason not to have to go on. Meat, to them, is what the writer calls ABCs. This is the extraordinary thing: we have them today. Meat, solid food, to many today is simply churning over the same old doctrines, congratulating one another how sound we are! And we think that is solid food! No! it is not, it is milk—ABCs.

I quote a commentator regarding this sixth chapter of Hebrews: 'If you brush off these solemn warnings, and imagine that they have no application to you as a believer, you may be at the very point of hardening your heart. We cannot escape the implication by applying it to others.' This is why many Christians are threatened by the view of Hebrews 6, that we are talking about saved people. The reason people do not want to think that those described were saved is very simple: they want to be able to be detached from those verses altogether. If they can just discuss them and say they are not talking about saved people, then there is no problem with the judgment seat of Christ, no problem with how they have to sort out their life, to come clean with God, to walk in the light, to forgive one another.

If someone can be satisfied that these verses are talking about unsaved people, that person does not even have to worry about it any more. To say that those described are unregenerate means there is no relevance for believers in these verses. But we need to let these verses operate on our lives, because, I believe, if it *does* grip us that those who were once enlightened, who tasted of the heavenly gift, who were made partakers of the Holy Spirit, and of the word of God and the powers of the world to come, *were* regenerate people, it is going to change everything. It is sobering but it will change our lives and spare us of needless agony.

The foundation

These Hebrew Christians wanted to keep laying the foundation. With every building there is a foundation and then the superstructure. What is the foundation? Paul tells us in 1 Corinthians 3:11, 'No one can lay any foundation other than the one already laid, which is Jesus Christ'. The writer said in Hebrews 3:6: 'But Christ is faithful as a son over God's house. And we are his house'. The foundation is there, and this is how a person is saved, and the ABC is simply the elementary things: repentance, faith, etc. But what about the house? You can build the house with wood, hay, stubble, or gold, silver, precious stones, and the day of judgment will declare what the superstructure is.

What does the writer say? He says, let us *leave* the foundation. There is a real danger that believers will just go back and forth *on* the foundation, calling it the deep things of God, meat and solid food, or catechism, or confession of faith, but never building the house, never doing anything that makes any impact on the world.

If Satan can divert us from the house, the superstructure, by keeping us laying the foundation again and again, he has won a major victory. He wants us to lay the foundation all the time, and the result: no relevance in the world, and Satan's territory is safe. Nobody is going to be invading Satan's territory because we are just laying the foundation again. But, the writer says, *not* laying again the foundation, let us leave, let us go on. This is what he wants to leave, so we can go on and build and build.

Before he proceeds, he does say what the foundation is. He lists six doctrines that he regards as foundational. There have been those who have made a big point of the fact that there were six. I do not know whether the writer was counting how many there were. I have a suspicion that he could have named six more; and yet because I believe in the infallibility of Scripture, and the writer was borne along by the Spirit, there is a pattern.

So we will deal in subsequent chapters with these six doctrines, although they are the very things he said that they must leave. But nonetheless he lists them and so we will see what they are. A simple outline gives not six but three points: how to be saved, how to grow and then eschatology.

Under saved he lists two doctrines: repentance and faith; under how to grow: baptisms and laying on of hands; and under eschatology: resurrection and the final judgment. Three categories, two for each. They are a summary of what all believers ought to know. It is possible some *would* be embarrassed to admit that they are not really at home with these three categories, and yet the writer says to leave them to one side.

The writer tells us what the foundation is, although he does not want the church to spend its years laying the foundation over and over again. Calvin said on this very point in his commentary: 'We must never abandon it, but it is ridiculous to spend all one's time laying it.' It is no sign that we love the gospel because we want to rehearse the ABCs over and over again. The more we aim at perfection, however much we come short of it, and we will, the clearer the gospel will be nonetheless. It is the person who is going on to maturity, not claiming to have arrived, but going on, who wants to please God utterly. To that person, the gospel, believe it or not, becomes clearer than ever, sweeter than ever, and the more one loves it, the more one will want to share it.

I heard Billy Graham tell this story. He said that a Methodist minister in America started having children's services at 10 am; the main service was at 11 am. At the children's service, he was just going to teach the very elementary things. After the second week, one or two adults went in; their excuse was that as they had to bring their children, they would just sit and listen. But the following week, two or three more adults came, and do you know, the 10 o'clock service got so big, it was bigger than the 11 o'clock service because the people really needed what he was giving to the children!

Could it be that we are not ready to go on to maturity, that we need the ABCs?

5

The Doctrine Of Salvation

Not laying again the foundation of repentance from acts that lead to death, and of faith in God (Hebrews 6:1b).

In the previous chapter I outlined, in three divisions, the six doctrines the writer listed. Repentance and faith I called the doctrine of salvation; baptisms and laying on of hands I called Christian growth; the resurrection from the dead and eternal judgment I called eschatology, the doctrine of last things.

The order of salvation
Under the doctrine of salvation, I am going to deal with repentance and faith. Since the normal scriptural order is repentance first (for example, in Mark 1:15, Jesus says, 'Repent, and believe the gospel'; Acts 20:21, Paul says, 'turn to God in repentance and have faith in our Lord Jesus Christ'; and in this verse here, 'repentance from acts that lead to death, and of faith in God'), a lot of people have asked why I have often emphasised faith as coming before repentance. When I did my research at Oxford, one of the things that I stressed, which was vital to my thesis, was how one looked at this would largely determine whether one agreed with my book on *Calvin and English Calvinism to 1647* (Oxford).

Calvin consistently emphasised that faith comes *before* repentance in the order of salvation. The reason Calvin stressed this is because of the way repentance was being defined at the time, namely, turning from any known sin. This is the way it was often done in the Middle Ages; some stressed what they called

'Preparation for Salvation'. Calvin was against that, and he said that we go straight to Jesus, looking to 'nothing but the promise'. So he insisted that faith goes before repentance. Now the reason he did that is because he knew that if you put turning from all sin before faith, then the person must have a change of life without any hope of the gospel.

The Puritans, after Calvin, often defined repentance as turning from every known sin. Now if you define repentance as turning from every known sin, and also insist that repentance must go before faith, then it means one must prepare oneself for salvation; a person must have a change in their life, someone must have a complete break from sin before they have even reached the place where they can even qualify for faith.

And that truly happened, and my thesis emphasised it, and I would not change a word of it, despite the attacks on it. I know that because some Puritans emphasised that a person could not come to faith until first they had turned from every known sin, there were people wondering whether they were saved. Those who had been taught this continued to doubt that they were saved. It is almost as though a person has got to be perfect before he can even be saved!

This is the background for the reason that I have emphasised that faith comes before repentance. I hope that it is clear and that one can see why. In other words if you are still going to define repentance as turning from every known sin, who will be absolutely sure he is saved? The gospel is that we go straight to Christ, and then from that we turn from every known sin in the process of sanctification.

Repentance

Why then, in building this foundation, would the writer say repentance first? There is no difficulty about that. The Greek word is *metanoia*, it means 'change of mind'. Repentance is agreeing with God; it is saying, I was wrong; it is simply changing the way you were thinking, which leads to changing the way you were living.

Now, the writer not only says, repentance, but he says repentance *from acts that lead to death*, a phrase that is only used again in Hebrews 9:14: 'How much more, then, will the blood of Christ, who through the eternal Spirit offered himself unblemished to God, cleanse our consciences from acts that lead to death, so that we may serve the living God!' What are acts that lead to death, or 'dead works', as the older translations say? The answer is: actions which anybody may have thought would help save them.

In the case of the Hebrew Christians, the fact that they were born Jews might have made them think that this must count for something. Or maybe the fact they had been keen to keep the law, and uphold the ceremonial law. Whatever. The writer is calling it acts that lead to death.

Paul in Philippians 3 said, 'I have got a pedigree that can upstage anybody.' But then he said those things which were gain he counted but loss. Why? They were acts that lead to death: of belonging to the tribe of Benjamin, of being a Pharisee of the Pharisees, of faultlessness in legalistic righteousness. In other words, dead works. Paul did not use the phrase, but that is what he meant.

Jesus told the parable of the two men praying in the temple. One, a Pharisee, said, 'God, I thank you that I am not like all other men'. He began to list various sins, and because he was not doing them, he thought that was endearing him to God. But his life was made up of dead works.

What could be acts that lead to death today? Well, we have the equivalents. A man who has been baptised as a baby or as an adult, who has joined a church and thinks that is going to help him. A woman who thinks that because she was born in a Christian home, that is going to help her. It is nothing but dead works.

So it is a phrase that probably had a meaning for these Hebrew Christians simply because of their Jewish background. But the equivalent would be anything, any work which we may have thought would endear us to God.

There is another interesting aspect of this repentance: repentance *from* not repentance *to*. There is no inference of having to do certain things before we can be saved. The first thing needed to be saved, and it is sufficient in itself, is that we come to the place that we know we are not worthy. We have nothing, we see that we have no bargaining power with God; we have nothing to give in exchange. That is repentance.

Another way of saying it is, *repentance is renouncement.* A renunciation of all that I thought would save me. Who knows, there may be somebody reading this who thinks that the way of getting to heaven or to having any kind of access into God's presence, or the basis of influence with him, is because of something you have done. You have tried to live a good life, you have tried to be moral, upstanding, and you are counting on these things. You will never be saved until you see that those are acts that lead to death. Repentance is here *from*, not repentance *to*; nothing is required, simply acknowledge you have nothing to give in exchange. As one hymn puts it:

> All the fitness he requireth,
> Is to feel your need of him.
> If you tarry 'til you're better,
> You will never come at all.

This is the gospel I have preached in Westminster Chapel since the first day I arrived, and I have not changed it one whit. It was offensive to some people who claimed to believe in free grace, yet I found that some people who use that term are often scared to death of it! To believe that you are saved by the death of Christ alone, there are not many people who really believe that. They say they do, and then insist that you need to have works to show it. Now, if you start taking that line where are you going to end? How many works? Are you going to start ticking them off? What do you need? Five? Ten? Fifteen? Twenty? A hundred?

This gospel is authentic. But repentance is just knowing you have nothing, nothing at all. This is so important! Although it is the ABCs, I think there are a lot of Christians who do not understand this, that a person is saved by realising that they have got nothing to bargain with. It is a change of mind.

By the way, it is something only God can do. Even though the word repentance is only used once by Paul in Romans (2:4), the way he uses it says enough: 'God's kindness leads you towards repentance'. It is a work of the Holy Spirit, and the Holy Spirit alone can bring a person to do this and to feel this way. As long as people still think that their works are worth something, they are still trusting those works! It is the work of the Spirit when you are not afraid to put all of your eggs in one basket: that Jesus did it on the cross, his blood atoned for our sins, that Jesus died for you. That is the work of the Spirit, and people are afraid to do that for they think there has to be some evidence of a change first. But the evidence is that you know you cannot save yourself. All the fitness he requires is to feel your need of him.

> In my hand, no price I bring,
> Simply to the cross I cling.

Later, in verse 6, the writer says that those who have fallen away cannot be *brought back* to repentance. Now why do you suppose he says that? Because he is talking about those who *had* already repented. A man or a woman cannot be *brought back* to repentance, if they have not once repented, if they have not come to the place that they knew they have got nothing to give in exchange. There had been a work of the Spirit, an operation of the heart, God's surgery on the soul. So there had been repentance in the first place. But the mechanism by which some of them perceived truth eventually snapped inside and they were not able to move on (Heb. 6:6). There was an arrested development; they could not grow in grace any more. And they were just not able to move on spiritually.

The ability to repent then must be given by God, but what the writer wants is that these Hebrew Christians would have a kind of heart that was teachable, warm, open, where there was a renewing of the mind as Paul said in Romans 12:2, 'Do not conform any longer to the pattern of this world, but be transformed by the renewing of your mind.'

The worst thing that can happen is that the Christian can never be renewed any more. It is a very sad thing and the writer does not want that. Instead, he wanted there to be a renewal, where one's heart is open, and can hear God speak. 'Today, if you hear his voice, do not harden your hearts' (Heb. 3:15). So the renewal of repentance is essential to the Christian, if he is to enter into God's rest.

Let me put it to you this way: here is the foundation. Once a person has repented, he or she is in Christ Jesus. No foundation can be laid other than what is laid, which is Jesus Christ. *But the only way that the superstructure can be built is that the person continues to hear the voice of God.* The maturity is where one is able to absorb solid food, where the capacity of the soul is enlarged to grasp things that come from God, which someone only hearing the ABCs all the time cannot handle.

I have preached a number of times on King Saul. Some believe that Saul was lost. Some have argued that King Saul was an example of the non-elect reprobate. I disagree. Saul was saved (1 Sam. 10:9). King Saul is an example of one who was illuminated but eliminated; who was brought to the place where he *had* tasted the goodness of the word of God and the powers of the world to come, but he fell away and could not be renewed again to repentance. King Saul later said, 'God is departed from me, and answers me no more.' When I preached on Ananias and Sapphira in Acts 5:1-11, many were shocked at first when I refused to say that these were unsaved people. Some would claim that Ananias and Sapphira were unsaved reprobates, and yet there is nothing in the New Testament that says that. Luke implies that they believed like anybody else.

Faith

On one side of the coin of salvation is repentance, on the other side is saving faith. You cannot have one without the other. It is not possible to have true repentance and not have saving faith or vice versa. So faith in God is exercised by one whose mind is changed and who has seen and embraced the promise. It would not be possible for a person simply to repent and then be in limbo. If God grants a person repentance, he will in that moment, give him or her faith. The work of the Holy Spirit never ends with repentance. So whenever there is repentance, there is faith. Where there is saving faith, there is repentance.

Why then does the writer say, Faith *in God*? This is interesting. He is talking to Hebrew Christians to whom faith seemed like something altogether new. It was something that was often controversial among the early Jews. Did you know the very idea of faith was considered strange? You say, How could they? Well, they did. They thought faith was something odd, although they had Genesis 15:6, on which Paul builds most of his case for faith. There was also Habakkuk 2:4, 'The just shall live by faith' that Paul uses in Romans and Galatians, and which is also used in Hebrews.

But faith, although it was in the Old Testament, was not exactly as prominent as the Davidic line, the kingship, the priesthood, the temple. That was what they were mostly interested in. Ceremony, circumcision, those were the things that excited the Jews. Faith was seen as a new idea. Do you remember, when Jesus was on the cross, the chief priests standing there shouted out, 'He trusted in God, let's see if God comes to help him!' Why did they say that? Well, it was obvious that Jesus was trusting his Father. Jesus had a perfect faith in God. Now that was unusual, and this was something they were using against him at the crucifixion. When we read it, we might think, why would they say that? Of course he was trusting in God. The reason it was said was because it was not done. What *they* did was to believe in the *ceremony*, in the *temple*, in the day of Atonement once a year, in their offerings and their sacrifices. The idea of faith in God apparently did not enter their minds. It was seen largely as a new idea.

The Jews to this very day do not have much concept of this

idea of faith. I was in Jerusalem a few years ago. As I alighted from a bus, a bearded orthodox Jew came up to me and said, 'May I say a prayer with you?'

I replied, 'You surely may. May I say one with you?' And he did not like the sound of that!

He asked, 'You want to pray with me?'

I responded, 'Yes, you said you want to pray with me, I want to pray with you too.'

He then asked, 'What are you going to say?'

I said, 'What are you going to say?'

He informed me, 'May there be peace in the world.'

I said, 'Is that it?'

'Yes.'

I said, 'You were going to pray with me.'

He said, 'I did—may there be peace in the world.'

I could see this man was pagan, there was nothing there. Little has changed.

Faith to many of us is something rather common. After all, it is the very foundation. But you have to remember that the writer, when he mentions this matter of faith, was having to show that it is not new, so that one reason for Hebrews 11 was to show that faith was not a New Testament innovation. The accusation could come: you are talking about faith all the time, we have not heard that before. So the writer says, You don't know about faith? Well, let me tell you. It was by *faith* that Abel did what he did (Heb. 11:4). Now it does not say that in the Old Testament but faith is what it was, says the writer. It was by faith that Noah did what he did. Genesis does not say it was faith, but that is what it was. It was faith that controlled and motivated all of these people and by the time he finished, they might say, 'Why have we not seen that before?'

Although we have had it handed to us on a silver platter, the writer of Hebrews was having to lay the foundation by talking simply about the very nature of trusting in God. Christians therefore are known as believers—people who have faith. The very act of repentance presupposes that one knew who Jesus was, that one was only saved by his death. The writer is showing the importance of repentance being that which made you say you did not have any ground to stand on except the righteousness that comes by faith. And it follows that you cannot have one without the other. Renewed repentance therefore will lead to an abiding trust. Repentance coming once put the person in the kingdom, and he was born again. Renewed faith means that one will build a superstructure.

6

Christian Blessing

Instruction about baptisms, the laying on
of hands (Hebrews 6:2a)

I know that when I first became the minister of Westminster
Chapel, some had fears that I was going to turn it into a Baptist
church. It is not in me to make this an issue, and I shall not do
so in this chapter. I might say some things that can be taken as
'Ah, there he is trying to say something or other' but no, I am not
interested in that. My background in America was in a church in
which there was a consensus from its inception that the two
things you would not divide on were baptism and eschatology.

The Church of the Nazarene was founded in 1908, and as I
understand it, there were three sections of the United States that
produced the charter membership: the north-east, around New
England; the south, Tennessee and that area; and California.
Those from California tended to believe in infant baptism and
post-millennialism, while those from Tennessee and the north-
east believed in immersion and were pre-millennialists. When
they met in Texas, they decided that they had too much in
common on the things that mattered to them to try to get
everybody right on those differences. So my background
tempered me to accept opposing beliefs on baptism and on
eschatology with great toleration.

Baptisms
The first thing that we must deal with is the fact that baptisms is
in the plural. The Greek is *baptismon*, genitive plural of baptisms.
This is what makes the verse a bit difficult to understand. If it

were in the singular, if it had said 'instruction about baptism', we would immediately understand that it simply meant Christian baptism, that is, when a person is baptised in or with water. But because it is plural it opens up the field, and there are no fewer than nine opinions as to what this means. We will look at them, but not in a way that will confuse you. I believe you will see that there is an element of truth to some of these which justifies the word being in the plural.

What about the word itself? The Greek word comes from the root, *bapto*, which simply literally means, to dip. For example, it is translated in John 13:26, 'Jesus answered, "It is the one to whom I will give this piece of bread when I have *dipped* it in the dish." Then, *dipping* the piece of bread, he gave it to Judas Iscariot, the son of Simon.' In Luke 16:24, in the parable of the rich man and Lazarus, the rich man looked up from hell and he asked Abraham to send Lazarus to '*dip* the tip of his finger in water...'. In Revelation 19:13, where the Lord is called King of kings and Lord of lords, he is said to be 'dressed in a robe *dipped* in blood'. That is the root word, *bapto*, and by the way those are the only three times it is used.

Then there is the word, *baptizo*, which is used 80 times. In the Greek it does mean to dip, or plunge, or immerse. I suppose that is one reason why in the Greek Orthodox church, even though they believe in infant baptism, they dip the whole body of the baby in water, because they must feel that is the only way you can understand baptism. In case you think I am going to take a strong view on immersion, I remember when I was in high school I was on a debating team. A debater learns how to debate both sides. For you that are a bit uneasy right now and might say, 'Well, there he goes with his Baptist views', the answer to that is what Jesus said, 'in a few days you will be baptised with the Holy Spirit' (Acts 1:5). The Spirit came down, so sprinkling demonstrates baptism —that is the other side. I thought I would show that I can take both sides in that!

Now, the noun *baptisma* is translated baptism. It is used twenty-two times, and simply means the ordinance of baptism.

But then there is another noun, *baptismos*, which is the act of baptism; it is only used four times. One of these is in Mark 7:4: 'When they come from the market-place they do not eat unless they wash. And they observe many other traditions, such as the *washing* of cups, pitchers and kettles.' That is our word, washing (of cups). It is used twice in Hebrews: 9:10, 'They are only a matter of food and drink and various ceremonial *washings'*. The other verse where it is used is 6:2, 'instructions about *baptisms'*.

Interpretations of baptisms

Firstly, John Owen said that because it says baptisms (plural), surely it is referring to many people being baptised. I do not think that many others have held that. Most people since John Owen regard it as a rather weak treatment of baptisms.

Secondly, a very common treatment is that it refers to the baptism of John over against the baptism that was instituted by the apostles. And indeed, as we read in Acts 18, there was Apollos, who had been baptised through the baptism of John the Baptist, and the twelve men in Ephesus who only had heard of the baptism of John and did not know that Jesus was going to baptise with the Spirit. In addition to the baptism of John the Baptist, there was that of the apostles in the name of Jesus. And so when the writer says 'instruction about baptisms' some believe that is what he meant.

Thirdly, there are others who think that because the writer was addressing Jews, they would have known of a pre-Christian practice, ceremonial washings that came out of the Old Testament. You find it for example, in Exodus 30:18ff, and we know that the Qumran sect at the Dead Sea, to whom some of these Christians could have had some connection, emphasised baptism. (Incidentally, you can go to the Dead Sea today and see the excavations of where they actually baptised.) So what the writer is doing when he talks about not laying the foundation again is simply trying to forget about all that. So that position would be that the foundation does not refer to Jesus Christ at all but simply to their Old Testament roots. Not too many hold to that but there is one respectable man who does, A. W. Pink.

Fourthly, some hold that the reason baptism is in the plural, is that there was a practice of triple affusion, that is sprinkling. The pouring of water was first in the name of the Father, second in the name of the Son, and third in the name of the Holy Spirit. Or if you believe in immersion, some think you could have been immersed three times. So since it was three baptisms, that was what was referred to by the writer.

Fifthly, another view says what might have been meant was a practice in the early church of preparation for baptism: there was a ceremonial washing on the Thursday but then on the Sunday the actual baptism in public. Therefore it was sort of two baptisms, and that is why the writer refers to baptisms in the plural. F. F. Bruce, who was a well-known scholar in this country, thought that this might have been what was meant, because he said that though this pre-baptismal baptism had no warrant in the New Testament, it may have been a legacy from Roman Judaism. Bruce thought that the Hebrew Christians addressed were in Rome, and that was why the phrase, 'about baptisms', was used.

Sixthly, Thomas Aquinas, the great Roman Catholic scholar, said that plural baptisms was used because there are three kinds of baptisms. There is baptism of water, there is the baptism of fire—of the Holy Spirit, and the baptism of blood—martyrdom. This became rather common in the Middle Ages. However, it probably was not common in the first century to talk about a baptism of martyrdom. Anyway it is not an uncommon view that this phrase refers to Christian baptism, the baptism of the Spirit, and the baptism of Suffering.

The seventh view is that of Augustine, who thought that baptisms was plural because there needed to be some distinguishing between the baptism of water, and what he called the 'baptism of tears', such being what would take the place of actual baptism if the water was not available, like the thief on the cross. So that if somebody were on their deathbed and received the Lord but could not be baptised, his tears would, as it were, take the place of baptism. I think that is a very sweet view, I am attracted to it, but I do not think that is what the verse means.

The eighth view is linked to Athanasius, who saw a lot of the wrong practice of re-baptising in his day, and so he thought the plural of baptisms had to do with the fact of people being baptised and baptised again.

The last view is that baptisms refers to the variety of causes for receiving baptism.

External and internal baptisms

Those are the nine positions that I have come up with. I would like to give a tenth. My view is, and I would not push it too far, that the writer is referring to Christian baptism and the baptism of the Holy Spirit. If you ask me to defend it by writing a 300 page thesis on it, I am not sure I could do it. But without superimposing it on you, let me state why I would hold that it refers to baptism upon profession of faith and the baptism of the Holy Spirit. Or, I would put it another way, it refers to an external and an internal: the baptism of water is external, whether you believe that it is by sprinkling or immersion; the baptism of the Holy Spirit is internal.

Now my reason is partly because of the order of the verse: repentance, faith, baptism. The person is saved by repentance and faith, then he is baptised following profession of faith. That seems to me to be reasonable. Then the baptism of the Holy Spirit is an internal seal upon what has taken place, a person having believed and repented, with the external baptism as the outward seal, the outward sign of an inward work.

As for the time the baptism of the Spirit takes place, I think you can make the case that in some cases it takes place at conversion; and in many cases, probably most, it takes place after conversion.

Remember how Apollos came and he was very fervent, speaking boldly in the synagogue, although not entirely aware of all Christian truth? However, Aquila and Priscilla recognised in him a man with potential, and they expounded the way of God more perfectly to him. It reminded me of the story of D. L. Moody, when as a young minister, he was pastor of a tabernacle. There were two women, the equivalent of Aquila and Priscilla, who sat down at the front, and when they went out the door and young D. L. Moody greeted them, they would say, 'Brother Moody, we are praying for you.' And the way they said it annoyed him. But what really galled him was that sometimes when he got up to preach, these two women would look at each other. And he did not get on too well with them. But one day D. L. Moody was going down the sidewalk in Brooklyn, New York, and suddenly the Spirit of God came down on him and his own words were, 'I literally begged God to stop it. I thought I was going to die right on the spot'; so powerful was God's presence. The following Sunday, when he got up to preach, before he said a word, those two ladies looked at each other as if they knew their prayers were answered.

Another reason for my view of this verse is because in Ephesians 4:5 we have the phrase, 'One Lord, one faith, one baptism'. That to me confirms that the one baptism of Ephesians 4:5 must have been external, for he is talking about salvation and baptism which is the external seal. Therefore, any reference to a second baptism certainly could not be anything that would militate against the one baptism of Ephesians 4:5.

Non-Trinitarian baptism

In the book of Acts there are baptisms in the name of Jesus, in the name of the Lord Jesus: Acts 2:38, 'be baptised in the name of Jesus Christ'; in Acts 8:16, they were 'baptised into the name of the Lord Jesus'; in Acts 10:48, 'in the name of Jesus Christ'. There have been those who believe that the only way to baptise, therefore, is not in the name of Father, Son and Holy Spirit but in the name of Jesus, or the Lord Jesus, or Jesus Christ. And there are still such today; I think most of them are Pentecostals. The more traditional denominations, until the Pentecostal movement, have followed Matthew 28, the Great Commission of Jesus: 'Go and make disciples of all nations, baptising them in the name of the Father and of the Son and of the Holy Spirit.' And as a consequence, for nineteen hundred years I should think, the church has baptised in that Trinitarian formula. But in the book of Acts it does not say that once, nor do you find it anywhere else in Scripture; and therefore there are those who would argue that if it is going to be a proper baptism it must be in the name of the Lord Jesus, or just in the name of Jesus Christ.

My view is that this is a technical point, of no great consequence. It is similar to the Lord's Supper. I know of churches that would argue whether you should use real wine or unleavened bread in the Lord's Supper. Churches have divided over this. I think we can get so technical, that we miss the whole thing.

Laying on of hands

This was something that was very common in the early church. Let us see if we can understand what is meant by the laying on of hands.

There is a little confusion here. Generally, baptism came before any laying on of hands, as for example, in Acts 8:16-17, 19:5-6, but not always. In Acts 9:17, Ananias laid his hands on Saul so that he might see and after that he was baptised.

Sometimes the Holy Spirit came upon a person through the laying on of hands, but there were other times when the Holy Spirit came down without the laying on of hands. For example, on the day of Pentecost, there was no laying on of hands, but the Spirit came down. In Acts 10, in the house of Cornelius, there was no laying on of hands; while Peter spoke, the Spirit came down, and they received the Spirit. But there are occasions when there was a laying on of hands, as we read in Acts 19:5-6, 'They were baptised in the name of the Lord Jesus. When Paul had laid his hands upon them, the Holy Spirit came on them, and they spoke in tongues, and prophesied.'

This matter of laying on of hands has roots in antiquity. It is a very interesting study, but I will give only a short survey.

Transfer of guilt

The first example that I have been able to find is in Exodus 29:10, and it is not laying hands on another person. It is when Moses directed Aaron and his sons to 'lay their hands on [the bull's] head.' In Leviticus 1:4, 'He is to lay his hand on the head of the burnt offering, and it will be accepted on his behalf to make atonement for him.' That signified a transfer of guilt to the head of a substitute. Glorious teaching! So the first example of the laying on of hands shows the transfer of guilt to the sacrifice. What happened when Jesus died for us is that all the guilt was put on him, and it was as though God laid his hand upon his Son, and he was indeed then smitten of God and afflicted. This is how a person is saved, realising that Jesus took all our guilt upon himself and trusting in him.

Consecration

The next example of the laying on of hands is in Leviticus 8:22, 'He then presented the other ram, the ram for the ordination, and Aaron and his sons laid their hands on its head.' In Numbers 27:18 the Lord says to Moses, 'Take Joshua, the son of Nun, a man in whom is the Spirit, and lay your hand upon him.' Here is a different usage of this matter. It is no longer a laying on of hands on an animal where you transfer guilt, it is a setting apart, a consecration.

Blessing

Then we find in the ministry of Jesus, 'Then little children were brought to Jesus for him to place his hands on them and pray for them. But the disciples rebuked those who brought them. Jesus said, "Let the little children come to me, and do not hinder them, for the kingdom of heaven belongs to such as these." When he had placed his hands on them, he went on from there' (Matt. 19:13-15). What we have here is Jesus laying his hands on the children, blessing them. Now what all that meant I do not know, whether when we get to heaven we will find those children having grown up and given a special ministry, and it is retroactive to that moment, or whether it was Jesus just giving his blessing. But I would not want to draw any more than that, except that Jesus did it, and there is a significance that he laid his hands on them.

Healing

In Mark 6:5, we find these words, 'He could not do any miracles there, except lay his hands on a few sick people and heal them.' In Luke 4:40, we read, 'When the sun was setting, the people brought to Jesus all who had various kinds of sickness, and laying his hands on each one, he healed them.' What we do know is that when it came to healing, he would lay his hands on people and they would be healed. But again, it was not the only way that he healed, sometimes he would just speak and it would be done.

Although laying on of hands was not the exclusive way of healing, it was a way. We know that with the apostles there was this laying on of hands. Earlier in the chapter I referred to the incident when Ananias laid his hands on Saul of Tarsus and he received his sight. In Acts 28:8, '[Publius'] father was sick in bed, suffering from fever and dysentery. Paul went in to see him, and after prayer, placed his hands on him and healed him.'

We would have to say that the ordinance of anointing with oil stated in James 5:14—'Is any one of you sick? He should call the elders of the church to pray over him and anoint him with oil in the name of the Lord'—is a method of healing.

Ordination

In the early church it was a kind of ordination. In Acts 6 deacons were chosen, and 'when they had prayed they laid their hands on them'. In Acts 13:3, we read these words, 'After they had fasted and prayed [concerning Saul and Barnabas], they laid their hands on them and sent them off.' In 1 Timothy 5:22, we find Paul referring to this practice when he said, 'Do not be hasty in the laying on of hands.'

When I was a boy growing up in Kentucky, the expression 'laying your hands on somebody' was a euphemism for fighting them. If you lay your hands on them, you go for them. As I grew up I would read that verse and wonder why Paul said, 'Don't do it suddenly.' Did you have to get to know them real well before you went for them?! But I grew up enough to realise that is not what he meant.

Not long ago, somebody, whom I had never met in my life, wanted me to sign a form saying they could be a counsellor at a Luis Palau meeting. I did not know this person, and this person was very offended that I would not do it. I said, 'You ought to go to a church where they know you.' The laying on of hands was done when ordaining a person, setting apart for the ministry, and one just did not do it to anybody who came along. Such had to be known fairly well.

7

The resurrection of the dead, and
eternal judgment (Hebrews 6:2b).

Eschatology

My task in this chapter is to give one semester of seminary training! That is right! In seminary one would take a whole semester, several months, to study what is called 'eschatology', the doctrine of last things. We are going to attempt it in one chapter.

Remember we are dealing with what the writer of Hebrews calls the essential teaching, the foundation. In the two previous chapters I dealt with repentance, faith, the doctrine of baptisms, and laying on of hands. Now I will deal with the last pair, resurrection of the dead and eternal judgment.

The New Testament preachers took these two things for granted. They went together, resurrection of the dead, and eternal judgment. They could not preach without bringing them in. Now the point is that there is life beyond the grave, there is judgment to come.

Every person will be judged, personally, by God Almighty. Maybe you have gone throughout your life and have never had any personal attention from anybody that matters, but you are going to receive personal attention from God. Hebrews 9:27, 'Man is destined to die once, and after that to face judgment.' This is elementary, but it is central Christian teaching. Yet how many believe this today? In the early church, they could not preach without mentioning this.

Apparently, these Hebrew Christians knew exactly what the writer meant, when he could just mention repentance, faith, baptisms, laying on of hands, resurrection of the dead, and eternal judgment, so he did not expand their meaning.

It is hard to know what was the consensus in the earliest church with regard to the Second Coming, whether they were pre-millennialists or post-millennialists. If this is new jargon to you, let me say that it is not of crucial importance; and yet sooner or later if you go into any study of the doctrine of the last things, you will be faced with this problem. In Revelation 20, there is a reference to Christ reigning for a thousand years, and the thousand years are called the millennium. Those who believe that Jesus will come before the millennium are called pre-millennialists; those who believe that Jesus will come after the millennium are called post-millennialists. Those who believe that the thousand years is a symbolic number and not to be taken literally are know as amillennialists. I often say, I am a pan-millennialist—I believe it will all pan out all right!

Resurrection of the dead
This phrase is found many times in the New Testament:

Acts 17:32; 'When they heard about the resurrection of the dead, some of them sneered, but others said, "We want to hear you again on this subject."'

Acts 23:6; 'Paul, knowing that some of them were Sadducees and the others Pharisees, called out in the Sanhedrin, "My brothers, I am a Pharisee, the son of a Pharisee. I stand on trial because of my hope in the resurrection of the dead."'

Acts 24:15; 'I have the same hope in God as these men, that there will be a resurrection of both the righteous and the wicked'; same chapter, verse 21, 'unless it was this one thing I shouted as I stood in their presence: "It is concerning the resurrection of the dead that I am on trial before you today."'

1 Corinthians 15:21; 'For since death came through a man, the resurrection of the dead comes also through a man.'

But there also is another phrase in the New Testament. It reads, the resurrection *from* the dead.

Luke 20:35; 'But those who are considered worthy of taking

part in that age and in the resurrection from the dead will neither marry nor be given in marriage';

Acts 10:41; 'He was not seen by all the people, but by witnesses whom God had already chosen—by us who ate and drank with him after he rose from the dead';

Romans 1:4; 'and was declared with power to be the Son of God by his resurrection from the dead';

Romans 4:24; 'But also for us, to whom God will credit righteousness—for us who believe in him who raised Jesus our Lord from the dead';

Romans 6:9; 'We know that since Christ was raised from the dead, he cannot die again.'

What is the difference? Well, we need to see that the difference is really crucial, and it is of extreme interest. The resurrection from, or out of, the dead means that there are others that are still dead, that will stay dead for a while longer at least. So that any reference to the resurrection from the dead means that one was called 'out of' death. The resurrection from the dead means that the others are still dead.

Hebrews 6:2 does not mention resurrection *from* the dead, it is resurrection *of* the dead. This is interesting and important because that one who was called the firstfruits of them that slept is our Lord Jesus Christ. He was raised *from* the dead on Easter Sunday, and that meant that the others who were dead remained dead.

This also means that if Jesus is called the firstfruits of them that slept, then he who was raised from the dead will be followed by a general resurrection of the dead. So the proof that everybody will some day be raised from death is that Jesus has already been raised from the dead. This is Paul's main point in 1 Corinthians 15:21-22: 'For since death came through a man, the resurrection of the dead comes also through a man. For as in Adam all die, so in Christ all will be made alive.' That term *made alive* does not mean that in Christ everybody is going to be saved. It is not referring to salvation. It simply refers to the fact of a general resurrection.

General resurrection

Some may say, 'Prove that there is a general resurrection.' Well, I will.

> [Jesus said] 'I tell you the truth, a time is coming and has now come when the dead will hear the voice of the Son of God and those who hear will live. For as the Father has life in himself, so he has granted the Son to have life in himself. And he has given him authority to judge because he is the Son of Man. Do not be amazed at this, for a time is coming when all who are in their graves will hear his voice and come out—those who have done good will rise to live, and those who have done evil will rise to be condemned' (John 5:25-9).

Yes, it is a general resurrection. So the resurrection of the dead, what the writer has mentioned in Hebrews 6:2, is everybody being raised. Other verses are Acts 24:15 and Daniel 12:2.

Now why is this important? Well, there are those who teach that those who are not saved just die, and will not be raised. They say it is only those who have been regenerated, born again, who are the children of God, who will be raised. And if you are not saved it means that after you die, you become nothing. You may not believe this, but there are Christians who teach this and claim to have biblical support for it. I do not think they have it. I believe in eternal punishment. I have been a Christian for nearly fifty years; I have been a preacher since 1954. If I knew of a way to avoid the teaching of eternal punishment, believe me I would. I do not say it is a sign of spirituality when I say that to you. Candidly, I wish it were not so. But I am compelled to teach it. There will be a resurrection of the dead that will include everybody.

Two-fold resurrection?

Yet the twentieth chapter of Revelation, a very difficult chapter, suggests two resurrections of the dead, which corresponds to 1 Thessalonians 4.

What was the issue in 1 Thessalonians 4? Let me try to explain it. There was a hope among all Christians in the years of

30-45 AD that Jesus was coming again. They did not expect to
die. Now, if you believed that you were going to live until Jesus
came again, it would be a good feeling. I think we would all like
that. I have met a lot of people over the years who believe that
God has told them that they will not die, that they are going to
be alive when Jesus comes. Well, I would like to believe that.
The point is that in the early church they all thought it. But then
people started to die!

In this church at Thessalonica, there was panic, they were not
prepared for this; the fear was, Well, what is going to happen to
our friends who have died? Paul wrote them this letter, and said,
'Relax, no problem. The Lord is going to come and those that are
asleep in Jesus are going to be the first ones to be raised. When
the voice of the archangel is sounded, the dead in Christ shall be
raised.' He did not say all the dead, but the dead in Christ shall
be raised. Then believers who are alive will be caught up
together with them, and they shall ever be with the Lord.

Now in Revelation 20, it seems there are two resurrections.
The first resurrection is what I just described from 1 Thessalonians
4. In other words, when Jesus comes, at his return the dead in
Christ shall be raised. I take this to mean what Revelation 20
calls the 'first resurrection', because John comments, 'Blessed
and holy are those who have part in the first resurrection' (v. 6).
But there seems to be a second resurrection in verses 12-13. 'I
saw the dead, great and small, standing before the throne, and
books were opened. The sea gave up the dead that were in it, and
death and Hades gave up the dead that were in them.'

At no point does the writer say this is the second resurrection.
Now if he had said that, we would have no problem, but he does
not say it. Yet the description in verses 12 and 13 seems to be a
second resurrection. I do not believe he would have used the
phrase 'first resurrection' if there was not a second resurrection.
When Jesus comes, and the dead in Christ are raised, that is not
only a resurrection of the dead, but it can be called a resurrection
from the dead, because it is leaving others.

When the writer in Hebrews 6:2 talks about the resurrection

of the dead, he does not say that there is a two-fold phase of this resurrection. But I think we must draw that conclusion.

Eternal judgment

The resurrection of the dead will mean that there is no human being that ever lived who will not be raised. And just as there is a two-fold aspect of the resurrection, there seems to be equally a two-fold aspect of judgment: there will be a judgment among those raised *from* the dead, a judgment of the saved; and then a judgment for those finally raised.

Those who have a part in the first resurrection will be judged as to the quality of their Christian living. When Jesus comes again, then there will be the judgment seat of Christ. 'Behold, I am coming soon! My reward is with me, and I will give to everyone according to what he has done' (Rev. 22:12). But that is not what the writer is referring to in Hebrews 6:2.

He is referring to the judgment at the great white throne: 'I saw the dead, great and small, standing before the throne, and books were opened. Another book was opened which is the book of life. The dead were judged according to what they had done as recorded in the books' (Rev. 20:12). The great white throne is not the judgment for those who are saved, but it is the judgment of the dead, because those who have been raised *from* the dead are already with the Lord.

At some other point in time, when I do not know, the resurrection of the dead, of those who are not saved, will take place. They will be judged out of those things which are written in the books. The conclusion will be that whoever is not found written in the book of life will be cast into the lake of fire. None of them had their name written in the Lamb's book of life. The issue of the great white throne in Revelation 20:12 is that of where will people spend eternity. Those who stand before God will be judged by their works—all those things that they have been counting on up to now to give a good chance of getting into heaven. God will not only show what they did but he will also reveal the selfishness and the sin and vileness behind it.

Annihilation

One last point. John says in Revelation 20:14: 'Death and Hades [hell] were thrown into the lake of fire.' The word for death in the Greek is *thanatos*. The word for the dead is *nekrous*. You say, What is the point? The point is this: *thanatos* is only translated one way and that is, death. *Nekrous* is translated one way, dead. *Thanatos* refers to a state or condition, death. *Nekrous* refers to corpses. Do you see what I mean? Death, a condition, is done away with, there is no possibility of death any more. It does not exist. As for the grave (Hades), that was also cast into the lake of fire. So after the great white throne, there will be no such thing as death or the grave.

It means that these people who have been raised up will live for ever and ever. There are those who hold the view of *annihilation*; they believe that when someone is cast into the lake of fire they will be burned up, that they become nothing, and that is the end of them. This is what the Jehovah's Witnesses teach, but there are also Christians who believe this, who do not want to believe in eternal punishment. Yet this is the awesome thing—the resurrection of the dead means that people will live for ever.

Hebrews 6:2 is not speaking specifically of the judgment seat of Christ. Why? Because he says resurrection *of* the dead, not *from* the dead. And the second reason I believe he is not speaking of the judgment seat of Christ, is because he wants his readers to leave the subject of judgment.

Part Two

God's Chastisement
Can Be Tough

8

The Sovereignty Of God

And God permitting, we will do so (Hebrews 6:3).

We are approaching the verses in Hebrews that have been regarded by some as the most difficult passage of the Bible, at least of the New Testament. For in them we have a description of people who were enlightened, tasted of the heavenly gift, made partakers of the Holy Spirit, tasted the goodness of God's word and the powers of the world to come, but who, should they fall away, could not be brought back to repentance. The reason for the difficulty is fairly obvious if you know any historical theology.

I have read over twenty commentaries on Hebrews and, as far as I am able to ascertain, there are no fewer than eight positions taken on this difficult passage.

Before I proceed, let me summarise. The writer is describing those who arrived at a certain state of grace, but then fell away. He says it is impossible for them to be renewed again, or brought back, to repentance. Now, why is this a problem? Well, if you are a Calvinist you are in difficulty, because Calvinists teach once saved, always saved, and these verses talk about falling away. If you are an Arminian, you are in difficulty, not because you do not say you can fall away, but I do not know of a single Arminian who says that if you *have* fallen away, you cannot be reclaimed, you cannot come back to the Lord! I do not know of a single Arminian who has taken this verse seriously. That is why it is difficult.

Various interpretations

Now of the eight positions that I have come across, one is the Arminian position, namely that those who are described here are saved, but that they lose their salvation.

And then there are four of the Calvinist position: one is that those who are described are saved, but the situation is only hypothetical, because of the word, if—'if' they fall away. That was Spurgeon's view. Secondly there is the position that those described in verses 4-6 have a non-saving work of grace in them, in other words they are not truly saved. That is the position of John Owen. The third position that could be called Calvinistic, is that the descriptions in verses 4-6 are of truly saved people, but if they did fall away it meant they were not saved after all. This is the position of Philip Edgecumbe Hughes, who has an excellent commentary on this letter. Or there is the view that those in verses 4-6 are saved but the falling away is not with reference to salvation, but to continued repentance. That is my own position.

There are three other views, and I would call them neither Calvinistic nor Arminian. One view is that the writer is only showing that the foundation cannot be laid a second time. Thus there is no such thing as a second repentance. That is the view of F. F. Bruce. Then there is the position that all it means is that no one can be restored while they are crucifying the Son of God afresh. In other words, as long as they are doing that they cannot be restored. So it is referring to a position of impossibility as long as a person is being that way, falling away, but he could be restored. And the last view is that the word 'impossible' was simply man's point of view, but not God's.

I think the reason I cannot accept any of these three views that I would call neutral, neither Calvinist nor Arminian, is because they do not do justice to the words, 'I declared on oath in my anger, They shall never enter my rest'. For that shows the impossibility is final.

So this passage has been a theological battleground for centuries. The fact that we are dealing with a difficult passage should keep us from being hot-headed or divisive. This passage has divided the best of God's people. All truth is revealed by the Spirit of God and each of us wants to feel that the Spirit has revealed it to us, we all like to think we are the ones that have got the answer.

We must remember that if we lose our tempers because others do not see it our way, then we betray our own insecurity and lack of confidence in the Holy Spirit. Ultimately, when we lose our temper, we are defensive, we are angry with God, because God has not shown the other person 'I' have got it right!

Truth is revealed by the Spirit. We can read various views, but one can only see anything by the Holy Spirit. Take for example, my own testimony. Back in 1955-56, the Lord revealed to me the doctrines of grace. I believe that the Lord showed me them, but there are Arminians who say, 'You just think the Lord showed you.' Well, I was satisfied the Lord showed me. I thought I had discovered something new, and that I was the first to see this. But I found out it was not new after all.

So again, what I am teaching is something so very clear to me, and I believe that the Holy Spirit revealed it to me. Again, I thought it was new, but it turns out that it is not. I discovered the Protestant Truth Society has a booklet taking the exact view I take, and that it was published years ago. For what it is worth, Billy Graham was curious as to my view of Hebrews 6. I told him my old view and what I believe now. He looked at me and said, 'Well, I have believed that for years, it is my present position.' So it is nothing new. The point is that a man convinced against his will is of the same opinion still. And the Protestant Truth Society booklet, if I had read it five years ago, I would have just put it aside, I would not have believed it.

Having said that, it makes it look like I think I have the truth. I earnestly pray I will not come across in that manner. If I tend to be dogmatic, do not let it make you feel uneasy, or do not feel you should not question what I say. Each of us must keep criticising himself right to the end. I do not have any desire to make anybody look stupid if they do not agree with me. Because whatever the truth is, God knows, and we must all say, 'Let God be true and every man a liar.'

The context is important

The context of this difficult passage is most crucial. There is the wider context and there is, of course, the immediate context. The wider context begins with chapter 2, when the writer says, 'How shall we escape if we ignore, or neglect, such a great salvation?' but chapters 3 and 4, the reference to God's rest, set the stage because what is referred to *as failure to enter* God's rest in chapter 4:1 is what the writer means by *falling away* in chapter 6.

By the way, I think that is a point that most commentators *are* agreed upon. Failure to enter God's rest is simply put in a different way in chapter 6:6, falling away is the same thing as failure to enter God's rest. That does not mean that they are all going to agree on what verse 6 means, but most are agreed that the failure to enter and the falling away are the same thing exactly.

The immediate context begins with chapter 5:11, when the writer says, 'We have much to say about this [Melchizedek], but it is hard to explain because you are slow to learn. In fact, though by this time you ought to be teachers, you need someone to teach you the elementary truths of God's word all over again. You need milk, not solid food!' The warning is that these people are dull of hearing. You know what it is like when a person goes deaf, physically, at the natural level. When this happens, the person has a hearing aid, and hopefully that will recover some hearing, but in some cases they go completely deaf. Now that is at the natural level; we all know about that. What the writer is warning about here is that a person can become dull of hearing at the *spiritual* level. And, alas, become stone deaf and therefore be unable to be renewed again.

What makes a person dull of hearing at the spiritual level? It is caused by neglect of the spiritual senses. In 4:12, the writer talks about the word of God, which is sharper than a two-edged

sword, and how it comes to judge. It is important for any
Christian that our senses are such that we can always hear God
speak, to have a heart that can hear the voice of God. If anything
were to happen that we don't hear as clearly, this is a warning
signal that we might go deaf.

But the problem according to this letter is that there is such
a thing as a deafness, spiritually, from which we never recover.
Just as at the natural level, a person can go deaf, but can still see
and do things, so it is with a person who is a Christian. He or she
can continue on except for one thing—God does not speak any
more, because there is something wrong in the heart.

The writer was warning these Christians that they were
already dull of hearing, and *that is the warning signal.* And yet,
he said to them, I do not believe that you are at the place where
you are in the description of Hebrews 6:4-6, where you cannot
be renewed.

That is the understanding that I have come to with regard to
this difficult passage. In other words, what these Hebrew
Christians had developed into was a place where they thought it
was simply enough to be sound theologically. This was the
problem. They believed that they could just keep on laying the
foundation. It was sufficient for them to hold to the truths, the old
doctrines, the faith, statements of belief.

But the writer says, 'Put that to one side. We do not need to
keep doing that again and again. There is something else that we
ought to be doing.'

The activity of the Spirit
Verse 3 is a most important verse, and if we do not understand
verse 3, we will not understand verse 4, I am certain of it. The
Greek for 'go on' is simply 'go on' and yet, that does not bring
out the full meaning. It is a Greek phrase that cannot be
translated with real meaning unless you add a lot of words. And
so, the phrase, 'God permitting', in verse 3, could be translated
as follows: 'God granting us mercy that we may be so enabled'.
That is my own translation. So it may be translated using the

parenthesis I suggested in previous chapters: verse 1, 'Therefore let us leave the elementary teachings about Christ and go on to maturity, and this we will do, God granting us mercy that we may be so enabled.' Why do I put it that way? Because 'go on' is in the verse that implies we cannot go on unless the Spirit comes behind and enables us to do it.

Enabling

Underline the word, 'mercy that we may be so *enabled'* . Why make this point? We need to see that we have here more than a pious cliché, like 'we will see you tomorrow, God willing!' That is not what the writer means here. We would miss his point if we thought that all he is saying is, 'God willing, we are going to do it'.

His point is, we will go on to maturity, to 'perfection' , God enabling us so to do. He is talking about entering God's rest, for it is an explicit reference to the sovereignty of God in bringing some, but not all, to his rest. God's *rest* and *perfection* are two words that may be used interchangeably, and on this point also, many commentators are agreed. That is the meaning of the verse. So we are talking about the sovereignty of God. Some will enter, some will not enter. The sovereignty of God must therefore be applied not only with reference to the saved and lost but also among the saved.

Having said some must enter, the writer in 6:9 says, 'Even though we speak like this, dear friends, we are confident of better things in your case.' In other words, he believes that some must enter and he has every hope for them, despite the fact that these Hebrew Christians were dull of hearing.

The rest is exactly what John calls 'fellowship with the Father'. It is what Paul called 'walking in the Spirit'. It is what Jesus talked about when he said, 'Take my yoke upon you and learn from me, for I am gentle and humble in heart, and you will find rest for your souls.'

Encouraging

Now verse 3 is not only an underestimated verse, but it is a most encouraging verse. It ought to uplift anybody who may be saying to themselves, 'You know, I do not believe there is any hope for me. I just do not believe I could ever enter into God's rest. I have been such a failure; I have been such a miserable Christian that there is no hope for me.'

Now the very fact that you could think like that shows that you can still hear! The problem is that some would be so dull of hearing that it would not even affect them. They would not even be bothered by this at all. In other words, there is still hope for those of us who have not been Joshuas, those who have not been Calebs. We have been on the fringes, we have never had great courage, but neither have we shown contempt for God's rest.

It is an affirmation then of the sovereignty of God, where nobody ever progresses further than the Spirit gives enabling grace for. So the writer will press hard for this maturity, but then he will warn against falling away. The very next words are a throwback to everything he has said just before. For at the end of the day, only God determines who enters into his rest. Just as it is true of conversion—it is the sovereign work of the Holy Spirit—it is equally true of entering God's rest.

Possible offence

There is a subtlety of offence in this teaching. I think there are many willing to speak of the sovereignty of God in conversion, but then they turn right around and want to deny the sovereignty of God with reference to entering his rest. But we know that when it comes to conversion a person is helpless unless God does it. And so with God's rest. We come boldly unto the throne of grace, that we may obtain mercy. Whenever we ask for mercy, it means we have no leverage, nothing to give in exchange.

When we come before God on our knees, we are aware that it is only by God's grace we have a glimmer of anything. We are aware that we cannot proceed unless God enables us. It is one thing to affirm the sovereignty of God at conversion, but are you prepared to do this when you are conscious that there is more that God wants to do in your lives, by recognising that this too is by sovereign grace? And should this be delayed in your own case, will you continue to affirm the same teaching?

9

The Reality of
the Impossibility
of Growth

[For] It is impossible for those who have once been enlightened (Hebrews 6:4a).

One might wish that the early church, which grew throughout the Mediterranean area in the first four centuries, had understood this verse in such a way that it was not possible for a misunderstanding ever to set in. But it is a sad fact that when we examine church history we are in for an appalling surprise.

I never will forget the feeling I had when I first began to read some of the Apostolic and Church Fathers. Apostolic Fathers would be those who lived in the second century, like Polycarp and Ignatius; the term Church Fathers is usually applied to people like Tertullian, Clement, and eventually Augustine. Apart from Augustine, many of these men did not have the theological grasp that we would suppose they should have had. Sometimes I think that because these men lived nearer to the time of the Apostles they would be right, but this is not the case. In fact, good men though they were, they did not have the theological grasp on elementary teachings that many have today, such as justification by faith.

There have been studies made in detail of the Church Fathers, and many scholars are surprised how little they understood. For that reason, Hebrews 6 gained a most unfortunate interpretation. Since the Roman Empire was Christianised in 312 AD, there has been a serious discussion as to whether it was truly Christian. What Constantine did when he became emperor, after he claimed to have seen a vision of the cross with the words 'By this sign you will conquer', was to make Christianity the legal religion of the empire.

But did you know that Constantine, even though he became a Christian, put off his baptism until just before he died? Why do you suppose he did that? It was because of the way Hebrews 6 was understood. They believed that any sin after baptism, such as adultery, meant that one lost his salvation and could not get it back. So people would delay their baptism, as if that was going to help.

There is a humorous interpretation in a letter called *The Shepherd of Hermas*. He had a 'new' understanding of Hebrews 6. Many believed that if they sinned after their baptism, there was not any hope, and many Christians were demoralised. But the Shepherd said that he had a fresh revelation from God. To all who had sinned since their baptism, 'God was giving one more chance'.

Many of us today have a much greater understanding than those men because we are thankfully in a post-Reformation situation.

Paul said there would be a falling away, and he wrote that in the 50s, and by the time you get to 100-125 AD, Christianity was anaemic in many, many ways. Do not think, in the twentieth century, that if you go all the way back to the second century, you are getting closer to the truth. It had degenerated almost to nothing but morality in many places, so that when they read Hebrews 6, it scared them all to death. But that kind of interpretation stuck, and even a man as learned as John Owen was still quoting Justin Martyr, another early Father, suggesting that enlightenment and baptism were used interchangeably.

It happened to others

The word 'for' found in most translations except the NIV, obviously shows the connection with the preceding verse, which is a reference to the sovereignty of God. There is no attainment without the sovereign will of God. Why this word, 'for'? What is the reason? Because *there is no automatic assurance that all who have been enlightened will enter God's rest.* As one commentator put it, 'There is at least a theoretical possibility that spiritual maturity may prove to be unattainable.'

The writer is saying that if that happened to others, it could happen to them. What did happen to others? Well, having been enlightened, having tasted of the goodness of God's word, having shared in the Holy Spirit, they did not enter into rest, they drew back, they came short, they fell away, and they could not be renewed. In verse 9 he says, he did believe it applied to his readers but he did not know for sure. For there *have* been those who fell away and did not come back.

What we have here is something that coheres with Hebrews 3, when the writer quotes God's words: 'I declared on oath in my anger, They shall never enter my rest.' In the Old Testament, once Joshua and Caleb were outvoted, nothing after that changed God's mind. Remember, we are talking about the children of Israel who kept the Passover, crossed the Red Sea, but who then started to complain about one thing after another. Moses would intercede for them, and God would forgive. This went on, and on, and on.

But the straw that broke the camel's back was when the spies were sent into Canaan. When they came back most of them said, 'We just can't do it! We can't go into Canaan, we are just grasshoppers and they are giants.' Caleb and Joshua said, 'We can do it. We can do anything with God's help.' But Joshua and Caleb were outnumbered, and everybody accepted the report of the other spies. None of these people entered into the land of Canaan. They all died in the wilderness except Joshua and Caleb. That is the background. And God said, 'I declared on oath in my anger, They shall never enter my rest.' This is why the writer of Hebrews now says, It is impossible. It follows, then, that any who are enlightened, but do not continue to walk in the light, can forfeit their inheritance just like that generation forfeited theirs.

Let us look now at this word, 'impossible'. In order to know how strong the word is, you need to know how it is used elsewhere. And we need not go outside this letter. The reason I am stressing this is there have been those who say it is impossible as long as somebody is not obeying the Lord. But I do not think we can agree with that view, partly because of what we know of the generation of Israel to whom God said, 'I declared on oath in my anger...'. In chapter 6:18: 'It is *impossible* for God to lie'; in 10:4, 'it is *impossible* for the blood of bulls and goats to take away sins'; in 11:6, 'And without faith it is *impossible* to please God'. In no case is there provision for compromise, the statements are all absolutes.

And so, we look now at the object of what it is that is impossible. We necessarily need to drop down to verse 6 to show that *the impossibility for those who fall away is that they be brought back to repentance*. We need to look at this carefully, calmly, without prejudice and simply read what it says. It is impossible for them to be brought back, or, renewed again, to repentance. Why do you suppose it says, 'back' or 'again'? Well, there is only one reason for that, that is, they had repented before.

There must come in every Christian a renewal of repentance, and this is something that will only take place as we walk in the light. Having been enlightened, we must walk in that light. It was a once-for-all experience; it happened, but one must walk in the light day by day. What happens if you do not? Well, if we confess our sins, we are forgiven; if we do not, then it means there is uncleansed sin, and the writer of the letter to the Hebrews says, 'If we deliberately keep on sinning ..., no sacrifice for sins is left' (10:26). When someone draws back, they do not walk in the light. Having come to the knowledge of the truth, he draws back, he sins wilfully. 'No sacrifice for sins is left.' It is so important that we do not let any accumulation of uncleansed sin dominate our lives for that can mean coldness will set in, and there will be a straying from the normal paths.

I am going to come back to this in a moment. But the point is, one must have a renewal of repentance, that is, we must be able to hear God's voice. We must keep our senses exercised to hear God speak. And as you walk in the light and you hear him saying, 'This is the way to go', then there will be a renewal of repentance. But if there is not a constant walking in the light, we are in danger of becoming hard of hearing.

What it is that is impossible for them to do

In a word, that to which they could not be brought back was the inward capacity to grasp God's call. They had lost the clear mind, having objectivity about things, lucidity. Truth escaped them, they could not find the handle as it were. They were people just tossed to and fro with no sense of direction. Remember the game when a person is blindfolded and asked to go in a certain direction? He (or she) starts walking but does not really know where he is going. Someone who does not walk in the light, is just like that. He is walking, he hopes, in the right direction, but he is not sure, and he is just trying to feel his way. A person who does not exercise the spiritual capacity to grasp the truth will be tossed about and will not have lucidity of thinking.

Let me put it another way: what does the person who cannot be brought back to repentance lose? The first thing is *discernment*. That is, the clear mind to make the right judgment. We use the expression 'presence of mind' to describe how someone knows just what to do in a crisis. There is nothing more wonderful than that. But to the one who cannot be brought back to repentance, there is no discernment and he is all at sea.

The next thing I would put is *equanimity*, evenness of mind. The double-minded will be unstable in all his ways (see Jas. 1:6-8). So to that one who cannot be brought back, there is no equanimity.

Another is *assurance*, and I do not mean here only assurance of salvation. What I am talking about is certainty, knowing that you have got it right. You can tell when you have got it right. When you are driving down a road, you know whether you are lost or not, you just feel certain. But the person who cannot be renewed again unto repentance has no assurance.

Fruitfulness: the one who cannot be renewed again will have no sense of being used in the kingdom of God. They might come and warm the pews, but they are not really fruitful.

Then there is the sense of *newness*, freshness, every day, of knowing that you are saved. That knowledge of being changed from glory to glory, God's presence and mercies new every morning. That has all gone.

Next, *enlightenment*. Jesus said, 'If the light within you is darkness, how great is that darkness.' And so they lose that.

Sensitivity. I refer now to being sensitive to God's voice, hearing him speak, that we can know when he is talking to us and respond.

The last loss is *sincerity*. That means a transparent honesty. We have seen people like this who, as they get older, sometimes lose all sense of honesty, and it does not seem to bother them. There are degrees of honesty, so there is the person who would not steal from another person, who would not rob a bank; but by honesty, I mean a transparent integrity, a sincerity that you are totally honest, with yourself, with truth, with people; there is nothing hypocritical.

How does one fall away?

I believe that this can take place in two kinds of situations: general and particular. I hope I can be clear here. Let me explain what I mean.

The *general*: what is that? It is when the whole lifestyle is incapable of any use to God ever again. That is what Paul feared in 1 Corinthians 9:27, when he said, 'I beat my body and make it my slave so that after I have preached to others, I myself will not be disqualified for the prize'; that he would never again be of use to God. There are other ways that this can be applied, but let me turn now to the particular.

The *particular* is when a special blessing is forfeited that can never be recovered. We have a scripture for this. In Hebrews 12:16-17, the writer says, 'See that no one is sexually immoral, or is godless like Esau, who for a single meal sold his inheritance rights as the oldest son. Afterwards, as you know, when he wanted to inherit this blessing, he was rejected. He could bring about no change of mind, though he sought the blessing with tears.'

During a sermon in my regular preaching, I mentioned this very interpretation of Hebrews 6. A professor from a college in Louisiana came up afterwards and said to me, 'You may be interested to know that the very position on Hebrews 6 that you are taking is what brought me into the ministry.' He told me how, when he saw that God was calling him to preach, that if he did not respond right then he would never again have an opportunity. He knew it, and it was this position that drove him to that. He knew that if he did not respond then, he could never be of use to God again in that way. How it was put to me I thought was very interesting: you can step out of the stream at any time, but you cannot step back into it in the same place. This is what I mean by the *particular*.

I told my congregation, that when I first heard of Evangelism Explosion, I fought it, spoke against it, and you know I forfeited something that I can never get back. I just thank God that he has given me a second chance. I believe that Jonah, had he gone the first time to Nineveh, would have gained something that he could never get again. Now it is true he went a second time—all things work together for good—and when they work together for good, it is so good you cannot imagine it being any other way. And so with me, I can now take advantage of the fact of the way the Lord has led me and I can say I know what it is to be a Jonah. And this is what I am saying: I know what it is to have God tell me what to do and not do it. But believe me, I forfeited something I will never get back again. That is what I mean by the *particular*.

The *general* refers to what happens after many years, till finally, and only God knows when this happens, there is the straw that breaks the camel's back, as it were. Like when Caleb and Joshua were outnumbered and the people wanted to go with the rest of the spies and said, 'We cannot do it.' God said, 'That does it.' I suspect that some Christians today have reached the place that generally never again can they be of any use to God.

The general is when the whole life becomes useless; the particular is when a situation itself cannot be redeemed.

10

The Experience Of Christians?

Who have tasted the heavenly gift, who have shared in the Holy Spirit, who have tasted the goodness of the word of God and the powers of the coming age (Hebrews 6:4,5).

In this chapter, we will look at the six descriptions given of these individuals who are said to have fallen away, and who cannot be brought back to repentance. We will be dealing with a passage upon which some have different positions. In chapter 8 I gave eight views that are held by evangelical, biblical scholars. I am making this statement so that you need not feel uneasy if you do not agree with me.

Now, it is obvious that the people described here are either saved or lost. The question is, which? The people described as (1) having repented, (2) who were enlightened, (3) tasted the heavenly gifts, (4) shared in the Holy Spirit, (5) tasted the good word of God and (6) the powers of the world to come—are they saved or are they not? Are these descriptions of truly converted people, or are they descriptions of the unregenerate?

A view that leads to being demoralized

I wonder how many have stopped to ask this question: if such people are *not* saved, when *will* they know that they *are*, if they want to be? Other than looking to Christ what should they look for to prove that they *are* saved? Because all believers, when they read this passage will think, 'I have been enlightened, I have repented, I have shared in the Holy Spirit. How do I know I am not an unsaved person if unsaved people can progress this far?'

Now if they were not saved, why would the writer tantalise us with possibilities that will demoralise us? If I find in these verses a description of myself, and then I learn that these people were never saved, am I to believe that *I* am not saved? How do I know for sure that I am? I have therefore concluded that the writer would not describe such people if he did not intend to encourage the rest of us. Surely this passage was not written to discourage us? Yet throughout my many years in the ministry I have known of many people who are afraid that they are going to *hell* because of Hebrews 6, for they fear they are in that category.

What signs are there by which I may conclude that I have been converted? Further, would such signs possibly exceed those already given in these verses? So if it can be said that you could have repented, been enlightened, tasted of the goodness of God's word and the powers of the world to come, shared in the Holy Spirit, and not be saved, then I ask, 'What *is* there that has happened to me so that I *now* know I *am* saved?' What, in other words, do we have to attain to so that we can finally know we are saved? If being enlightened is not enough, having repented is not enough, shared in the Holy Spirit is not enough, then, what can we have whereby we may know that we are saved?

I say this to show why I have come to the conclusion that these are saved people, because surely the very signs people want, in order to believe that they are saved, *could not possibly exceed* the very ones given here. In other words, if they were to discover that they have not been converted, the very evidences they *would* seek so as to be truly converted would surely be these six very descriptions!

This is one of the reasons why there are those in the Reformed tradition who are not sure they are saved. And it is this line of thinking that has precipitated an uneasiness with many sincere Christians so they do not have assurance of salvation. I have been convinced for many years that it is the devil's wish that Christians would always be bothered by the problem of whether they are saved, so that they will *stay* in that condition, and never be of any use to God. As long as people are still wondering whether they are saved, they are not going to do anything. The years go by and they say, 'Oh I would love to do something for the Lord, but I am not sure that I am saved.' And after all, if these people described in Hebrews 6 are not saved, despite having all of these spiritual attainments, we can understand why some godly people still say, 'I might not be saved, because those in Hebrews 6 were not saved.'

Pastoral reality

I will make another observation. There have been hundreds of thousands of people who, realising their hypocrisy and their superficiality, have been awakened, and come to repentance. We all know this to be true. But to say that people who have had a taste of the Spirit's work and remain unconverted cannot be converted, is to go right against all pastoral experience. Someone will say, we should not go by experience, we should go by the word of God. But at the pastoral level the Bible does not want to demoralise us, it wants to encourage us.

Wherever I have found a Reformed or Arminian minister, they do not acknowledge at the pastoral level that there is a person who has no hope of salvation, even if they have been converted and sinned. They always say to such people, 'Well now, how far have you come? You were once converted or you professed faith in Christ? Yes? What has happened since?' 'Well, the years have gone by and I have fallen into deep sin, I have renounced the church and I have done everything that is against what God wanted me to do. But now, I would like to get right with God.' What do we do with people like that? Do we say, 'Sorry, there's no hope?' No. We accept them, and lead them right on to the Lord. I do not know of a single Reformed or Arminian minister that is any different.

There is an interesting possibility in the text, which I am not going to push too far, and it is this. At the beginning of chapter 6, the set of doctrines, which we saw are called the ABCs, are listed in this order: repentance, faith, baptisms, laying on of hands, resurrection and eternal judgment. So at the beginning of the chapter there are six doctrines and then in verses 4-6 we have six descriptions. I think that it is not accidental. Repentance corresponds to repentance, that is obvious; enlightenment, I believe, to faith; the heavenly gift to baptisms; the Holy Spirit to the laying on of hands; the word of God and resurrection does not quite match and for that reason I am not going to push it too far; but then the powers of the coming age to eternal judgment. And so, apart from the one exception, there is possibly a connection between them.

As I dealt with repentance in chapter 6, I will not repeat what I wrote there. If asked, where is repentance found in these descriptions? It is in verse 6 where being 'brought back to repentance' shows what they had personally experienced. Here are the others.

Enlightenment (illumination)

The Greek verb is *photisthentas* (illuminated). It is the verb form of *phos* (light) which is used seventy times in the New Testament. Paul uses it in 2 Corinthians 4:4, 6: 'The light *(photismon)* of the gospel of the glory of Christ, who is the image of God. For God, who said, "Let light *(photismon)* shine out of darkness", made his light shine in our hearts to give us the light of the knowledge of the glory of God in the face of Christ.' The verb form, *photizo*, to illuminate, is used eleven times. It is used in Ephesians 1:18 where only saved people can be meant. Only once is it used to describe all men, and that is in John 1:9: those who want to make the case that Hebrews 6 is describing graces of those not really saved, point out that the same word is used in John 1:9 and they say, 'The word is used there, and that shows that it need not mean that a person is regenerate.' What is the answer to that?

They overlook this Greek word, *apax*, that is translated 'once' in Hebrews 6:4, but many times it means 'once for all'. It is exactly the same word used in Jude 3, 'the faith that was once for all entrusted to the saints'. The word, once for all, is a favourite of the writer of Hebrews. For example, Hebrews 9:27, 'Just as man is destined to die once, and after that to face judgment, so Christ was sacrificed once (for all) to take away the sins of many people.' So, we not only have the word which means enlightened, but the writer says it was a once for all enlightenment. Why? Because they had been converted. That is what is said of these people.

Tasted of the heavenly gift

The Greek word is *geuomai*, taste; it is the Greek word that means *experience*. It is translated 'ate' in Acts 20:11. It is used fifteen times; five of those are with reference to death. I used to believe the well-known comment of Matthew Henry, one can taste something without digesting it. I would use illustrations of different kinds of food that you can taste without digesting.

Then one day somebody pointed out to me that in Hebrews 2:9 it said that Jesus tasted death. I said that it must be a different Greek word! My heart started beating really fast, and I turned to it and thought, 'Oh no, same word!' So my argument fell. The word can mean 'eaten', and it is used by Peter in 1 Peter 2:3, 'now that you have tasted that the Lord is good.' It is an actual experience. The 'heavenly gift' is surely the Lord Jesus! It is the gospel, the forgiveness of sins.

Shared in the Holy Spirit

Now there are two words here, *metochous genethentas* ('made partakers', AV)—'shared in the Holy Spirit': it is an aorist passive participle, they were 'made sharers' in the Spirit. It is a word that is sometimes used to refer to a partnership. The same writer in Hebrews 1:9 says, 'God has set you above your *companions* by anointing you with the oil of joy.' It is the same word as we have here in Hebrews 6:4, translated 'sharers', partners. What does it mean?

It would seem to me, minimally, to mean regeneration. Anybody who has shared in the Spirit, at the least the work of the Spirit has illuminated him, by producing faith. But maximally it could mean, and there are those who hold to my view and make a big point of it, that it refers to somebody having been baptised with the Holy Spirit and even experiencing the various charismatic gifts of the Spirit.

I suspect that the writer wants to go beyond simply saying that the person has repented, and he is describing a Christian who has gone on *quite a way* with the Lord. We may not be referring therefore to a person who had been converted and then six months later gets discouraged. It may be describing somebody who has experienced more than simply being baptised; that would be the implication of the word, that this person has gone on with the Lord, experiencing even the baptism of the Spirit, having certain gifts. But I am not going to push that point. Minimally, surely, it means regeneration.

Tasted the goodness of the word of God

We have already dealt with the word, taste, so we will just go on. The Greek word here for 'word' is, *rhema*, not *logos*. That in itself does not prove anything. There have always been biblical scholars who want to make a big point about *rhema* and *logos*. But the argument falls flat when we realise that it can be shown that these words are sometimes used interchangeably.

Yet it might be that the writer chose *rhema* to describe a word from God in terms of an 'utterance'. There were those who had tasted the good word of God in that maybe somebody had made a prophecy concerning them. Or they felt God spoke intimately to them. Another might say that this is simply a reference to the fact that we have tasted of the goodness of God's word in that we know we are going to be raised from the dead some day, and it is good news.

Now the difference between heavenly gift and the good word of God – the possible connection I mentioned earlier in the chapter – may mean that the heavenly gift used earlier is a reference to Jesus and the gospel, and the good word of God refers to our hope of eternal life. But beyond that I do not know that we can be certain as to what is meant by the goodness of God's word. It is almost as though the writer is repeating himself here. Why say 'the goodness' of the word of God? Can it be anything else? But that is what he said, and I could give you various scholarly interpretations but I do not think any of them prove very much.

Powers of the coming age

This most certainly refers to the future, and does seem to link up with the sixth doctrine stated earlier—eternal judgment. What does it mean? Well, I would say minimally, it refers to having assurance of final salvation. So if a person has tasted of the powers of the coming age, he knows now how it is going to be at the judgment. That means that those described in Hebrews 6, who fell away, were not only saved, but had a high degree of assurance of their salvation. I suggested earlier that they had even experienced deep things of the Holy Spirit which shows they had gone on with the Lord indeed in a wonderful way.

What else could it mean? Well it could mean that a person had assurance of the very reality of Christ's coming. Now I am going to give a personal experience, not always a good thing to do, for it could be dangerous, but I do not believe in this case it will be.

Many years ago, back in 1955 to be exact, a few days after I myself had what I have described as a 'Damascus-road' happening, I had an experience one evening which lasted for maybe an hour, when the second coming of Jesus was very, very real to me. That is the only way to put it. I commented to my roommate in college on how real the second coming of Jesus was. He said, 'Well I know that, the Bible says so.' What I meant was a powerful witness that Jesus was coming again. So much so that I wondered if he was going to come in a day or two, it was that real.

All I am saying is that I had the experience many years ago, it did not last long, and I have not had it since. Yet it made me wonder that what I experienced may be partly a description of what the writer means by 'tasting the powers of the coming age'. In a word, we are describing the experiences of life beyond the grave, the reality of heaven beyond the present age.

11

Falling
Away

[It is impossible...] if they fall away, to be brought back to repentance (Hebrews 6:6a).

We may well wonder why the Holy Spirit left to the church such a difficult passage of scripture as Hebrews 6:6. Yet I know that when we get to heaven and God gives us the undoubted explanation, we will say, 'Well, of course! How blind we were.' Whenever God reveals something, it is always in such a way that we say, 'Why didn't I see that it was so obvious?' Mind you, just because it is obvious to you, it does not mean it will be to everybody else. It is hard to believe that the doctrine of justification by faith alone could have lain hidden from the church generally for nearly fifteen hundred years. And having seen what Luther saw, we say, 'Well who would doubt that?' But the point is that there were those who did not agree with Luther.

Now we do, however, have a most difficult passage here. It is a fact that the church, as far as I know, has never resolved this, and is likely to remain divided.

I mentioned in Chapter 10 the opinion of Hermas, who wrote a treatise called *The Shepherd*, in which he wrote that God said you can sin after baptism and not be forever lost. He gave everybody 'one more chance', because Hebrews 6 had swept around the churches, and everybody was in despair. Hermas had the vision that everybody could have one more opportunity. And some people breathed easier. As I told you, Constantine delayed his own baptism until just before he died, as if that was going to help. He wanted to be sure that once he was baptised, he would never sin again.

After the Reformation came and the light of justification by faith turned the world upside down, there were still differing interpretations. The Arminians claimed that this passage proves that you can lose your salvation, but then they avoided the passage like the plague because they did not want to face the impossibility of a person being restored. And as I said in Chapter 9, there are eight different interpretations that I know of.

In this chapter we go straight to the heart of the matter, and the first thing we have to deal with is the word, 'If'— *if* they fall away...' It is a fact that there is no 'if' in the Greek. What the Greek says is *parapesontas*, 'And having fallen...' That is exactly the way it reads. There is no 'if' at all. If you refer to a Revised Standard Version or a New English Bible, you will see that they translate it just like it is, 'They fell away'. The New American Standard Version says 'having fallen away...' So there is no 'if'. But the Authorised Version and the New International Version say 'If...'. That is how Spurgeon explained the verse. He said, 'It says *if*, thank God it has never happened yet.' Spurgeon had no doubt it *was* describing Christians! He just said it did not happen. But there is no 'if' in the Greek at all.

However, the NIV has put the 'if' there. Now why did they do that? Well, I know of three possible reasons. The first is that the tense is the aorist participle which in a grammatical context as we have here, may sometimes imply an 'if'. That is, it could easily be used in a conditional sense, so it is not a grammatical error necessarily to have the word 'if' there. The second reason the NIV could have put it in is because the 'if' does not take away the awesomeness of the warning. The third reason is that the NIV had a vast constituency of evangelical translators from all denominations, both Arminian and Calvinist, and they had committees to deal with this verse and so they were conscious that, although they would not compromise, they needed to have a version that would have vast appeal.

Now *parapesontas* is the accusative plural, masculine gender and aorist participle of *parapipto*. You can translate it either 'fell away' or 'having fallen away'. It means that it is something *that had already happened.* It is not a hypothesis. Some had fallen. One difficulty that we have here is that this particular word *parapesontas (parapipto)* is nowhere else found in the New Testament. That means we do not have any other verse we can compare *parapipto* with to see how it was translated. So what one does in a case like this is to see how the word was used in ancient Hellenistic literature. If you find it, and see how it was translated and used, you can assume how it would have been used in the koine Greek, and understood by these Hebrew Christians.

According to the scholars, *parapipto* means literally, to fall aside, or fall alongside, or fall beside. But had it been translated, 'those who fell aside', it would not sound right. 'To fall away' probably reads better. However, to say that they fell *away* is possibly really stronger than the word meant to convey.

I can give you an example of how a translation can imply something far more than the word intends. For example, in 1 Corinthians 11:28 in the Authorised Version, Paul says, Let a man examine himself and he that partakes unworthily drinketh *damnation* to himself. The Greek word is *krima*, which means 'judgment'. Nine out of ten times that is the way it is translated in the Authorised Version. Now had it read 'he that drinketh unworthily, drinks *judgment* to himself', we can see that that is still serious, but it does not quite give the feeling that it is necessarily damnation. See what I mean? I am just showing that the way a word is translated will imply a meaning; and there are many people who to this day are scared to partake of the Lord's Table lest they eat and drink damnation, because they are not sure they are worthy. The word there is *judgment*, and the judgment may or may not mean condemnation. Obviously it could simply mean that you are going to receive God's chastening. And the judgment that you bring upon yourself does not mean that you are going to go to hell at all, but it means that you might bring chastening, because Paul went on to say, 'That is why many among you are weak and sick, and a number of you have fallen asleep'. My point is to show how a word, by the way it is translated, can imply something worse than it really is.

There is another thing that I think will be of interest to you about *parapipto*. If you take away the word *para* you have *pipto*, and that simply means 'to fall'. The word *para*, in the Greek, always means 'aside'. For example, the word that many will recognise, *parakletos, paraclete*, the Comforter, the Holy Spirit, is 'one who comes alongside'. So our word comes from *parapipto* which means *fall aside*.

Now the reason I am going into some detail here is to show that there are times when *pipto* alone is used—it has actually been used three times in this very letter—and there is some reason to believe that adding *para* to *pipto* weakens rather than strengthens the verb. If it is a fall, then it is full stop; but to fall aside could mean simply a deviation. I am not making a case that that is the *truth*, but I think a Greek scholar would agree that adding *para* to the word could weaken it. However, there are other places when only *pipto* is used, and it just means fall:

Hebrews 3:17, 'And with whom was he angry for forty years? Was it not with those who sinned, whose bodies *fell* in the desert?';

Hebrews 4:11, 'Let us, therefore, make every effort to enter that rest, so that no-one will *fall* by following their example of disobedience';

Hebrews 11:30, 'By faith the walls of Jericho *fell*, after the people had marched around them for seven days';

Revelation 1:17, 'When I saw him, I *fell* at his feet as though dead';

1 Corinthians 10:12, 'So, if you think you are standing firm, be careful that you don't *fall*!'

What I am showing here is that our word *parapipto* comes from *pipto*, but take off the *para* and you have got *pipto*, a word used ninety times in the New Testament.

Let me show you another interesting aspect of Greek. There is another word *ekpipto*, used thirteen times in the New Testament. *Ek* means 'from' or 'out of', so that whenever we have *ekpipto* it is to 'fall *out of* or *from*'. For example, in 2 Peter 3:17, Peter says, 'Therefore, dear friends, since you already know this, be on your guard so that you may not be carried away by the error of lawless men and *fall* from your secure position.' Here it is *ekpipto* and there is a sense in which that is a much stronger word than *parapipto*. I will not push this point because in a way it does not matter, I am just letting you see that we are dealing with a Greek word here, that in and of itself does not prove a lot, except that we are obviously talking about some kind of deviation from the straight and narrow. And one other example where *ekpipto* is used is Revelation 2:5, and I find this very, very, very interesting: 'Remember the height from which you have *fallen*! Repent and do the things you did at first. If you do not repent, I will come to you and remove your lampstand from its place.' That is the word *ekpipto*. What is interesting here is that when *parapipto* was used in Hebrews 6:6, it says you could *not* repent. Now it is *ekpipto,* which I think is probably a stronger word, yet Jesus commanded the church in Ephesus to repent! Obviously there was hope.

Now I want to show you another thing. Hebrews 6:6 says, 'if they fall away, to be brought back to repentance.' Could it be that such people had on previous occasions fallen and were renewed? But perhaps they had done that too many times, so that now they *cannot* be brought back. It would seem they were like those in the wilderness for forty years, when God said, 'I declared on oath in my anger, They shall never enter into my rest.' Perhaps they had been warned before and then they repented, and then they fell, and then they were brought back, and then they fell, and they were warned, and they were renewed, until something happened, and the writer brings in this word, *palin* (again). The Authorised Version brings this out forcibly: it is impossible for them to be renewed *again*, implying they had been renewed before at least once. Interestingly the word translated *again* in the Authorised Version is found 142 times in the Greek and each time it means 'again'.

I would point out that the word *renewed* is sufficient if all the writer is saying is that those who fall away cannot be renewed unto repentance. Why did he say they cannot be renewed *again* unto repentance? For the renewal implies that there had to have been a falling of some kind or there was no point in phrasing it as he did. The word *renewed* is a word that is complete in itself, and shows that there had been a once-for-all repentance; but the expression, 'renewed again' or 'brought back', implies that they had been renewed before but that they fell again. In other words, the writer must have had specific persons in mind. And these persons had more than once, for all I know, brought disgrace upon the Christian church. Hence this expression, 'Put him to an open shame.'

I have been preaching now since 1954, and I can think of many examples of people that have brought the name of Christ into open shame during that period. You can probably think of people too. You may know of somebody right now who, by the life they are living, brings the name of Jesus into open shame. Yet you would not say, 'Well, I don't think they can ever be restored.' The chances are you would say, 'Well, I believe they could be restored if they repented'; you pray that they will be renewed. Sometimes they do come out of it!

Biblical examples

Let us look at it another way. The possibility of repentance after falling is seen many times in the Bible. Why, all of a sudden, would we have a reference to somebody who falls aside, or who falls and who cannot be renewed? What have they done that is so bad?

Look at *David* who committed adultery and then murder—if that is not falling I do not know what is! But Nathan the prophet went to David and, although he was very self-righteous for a while until he realised that he was guilty, he said, I have sinned. And David was brought back to repentance.

Remember *Jonah*. God said, 'Go', but Jonah said, 'No'. God came to Jonah a second time. Jonah was renewed. But I have thought, and I cannot prove this point, that if Jonah had not gone the *second* time, he possibly could not have been renewed *again*.

Take *the incestuous man in Corinth*. In 1 Corinthians 5 the apostle Paul writes a letter to the congregation. How he must have felt! He hears that among his own converts at Corinth there is a man living, sleeping with his father's wife, probably his stepmother. Paul says that is a sin of a kind not found even among pagans. So Paul delivers him to Satan. Paul just writes him off; he forgets him. But do you know, when the man heard what Paul had done, he was shattered; he was so sorry, I dare say he wept and wept. He was restored. The point is the man fell. He was renewed, if as P. E. Hughes believes, he is referred to in 2 Corinthians 2:ff.

Look at *2 Timothy 2:25-26*: 'Those who oppose him he must gently instruct, in the hope that God will grant them repentance leading them to a knowledge of the truth, and that they will come to their senses and escape from the trap of the devil, who has taken them captive to do his will.' Paul does not deny the possibility of being brought back to repentance.

When you read Hebrews 6, how bad must a person be in order to commit that sin? Do you think there is anything worse than David's sins of adultery and murder? Well, he was renewed. Here was Jonah, disobedient to the mandate to go to Nineveh, he was renewed. Peter denied the Lord after following him for three years, when he let a little servant girl accuse him and he denied the Lord; he was renewed. The man who committed incest, he was renewed. I ask how bad do you have to get, so that you cannot be renewed?

1. There are degrees of falling away
All of us have done this at one time or another. If there is anybody who has not sinned since they professed faith in Christ, please go to a photographer and have a picture taken of you and your halo! We have all sinned. Who among us has not? There are degrees of falling away. But we know that God is merciful.

2. Once a person has fallen away, God is not obligated to grant repentance

Now I would define falling away as simply sinning without any repentance. Some sin and then they repent. Some sin and a month later they repent. Some sin and a year later they repent. And I would have thought that a fall often means the person who sins is not too bothered by it at first. Now here is the point: once a person has fallen, that is, he or she sins and does not repent, God is not obligated to grant repentance. For something is lost, something is forfeited when we sin. I believe that if a person sins without repenting very quickly, he loses a certain spiritual autonomy. For example, Romans 12:2 says, 'Do not conform any longer to the pattern of this world, but be transformed by the renewing of your mind. Then you will be able to test and approve what God's will is—his good, pleasing and perfect will.' When a person realises right away that he has sinned, and wastes no time in saying, 'God, I am sorry', then there is virtually an unbroken fellowship. But to the person who sins and does not immediately repent, he loses a certain autonomy, and God might not grant him repentance.

3. You can step out of the flowing stream, but you can never step back in at the same place

Those described in Hebrews 6, I believe, were in that situation because they spurned the opportunity to repent too many times. So what we have in Hebrews 6:6 is what I would also call *terminal chastening*. It is the last resort. It is what John will call at the end of 1 John 5, the 'sin unto death'. The crucifying Christ afresh is a reference to our sin bringing disgrace upon him. He died for our sins and therefore when we confess our sins, it surely goes without saying we are going to live to please him; but when we sin, we put him back on the cross again. And that is what is meant by crucifying him afresh. It is a word that means 'recrucifying'.

4. This is not the blaspheming of the Holy Spirit

Not at all. The blaspheming of the Holy Spirit cannot be committed by a Christian, and those described in Hebrews 6 were in my view regenerate, they were saved. And they will be saved as by fire, for the fact that they fell implies that there was a height to fall from!

Why these described in Hebrews 6:4,5 could not be renewed, then, seems to be explained by these references we had in chapter 3, when God said, 'I declared on oath in my anger, They shall never enter my rest.' God is patient, and he has been patient with all of us. I cannot prove what I am about to say, but I believe it. There is probably not a single person reading this book that is described by Hebrews 6:6. Could be, but I doubt it, because I do not think otherwise you would be reading this book. This extreme situation of Hebrews 6:6 is when people have gone so far that God just washes his hands of them, like the spies who outvoted Caleb and Joshua in Numbers 13:31-33. They had seen the glory of God ... the Passover, the pillar of fire, the crossing of the Red Sea. But they drew back from God's mandate to enter Canaan ... an insult to God.

Yet there *is* always the possibility that what happened to those who were enlightened, tasted of the heavenly gifts, could happen to us. It is just a reminder that all of us are dependent upon God's sovereign mercy, and if the great apostle Paul who was as spiritual, I guess, as any man that ever lived, could nonetheless say, 'so that after I have preached to others, I myself will not be disqualified for the prize', how much more should we?

So what the writer has done is to say that 'we will go on to maturity by God's enabling grace', and then he reminds us there are those who cannot. That is why we all can be thankful if we have been spared, and that we have a heart that is warm and docile, and wants to please the Lord.

12

Recrucifying Jesus

Because to their loss they are crucifying the Son of God all over again and subjecting him to public disgrace (Hebrews 6:6b).

Now the position that we have come to see in this passage is that the writer is describing those who are truly converted. They are saved, and their falling is not with reference to salvation. It is with reference to being renewed again to a God-owned change of mind. What the writer says is that it is impossible for these particular Hebrew believers to be renewed again. He knew who these people were. They had been renewed before, how often we do not know. But the point is, they had gone too far and they could not now be brought back to God-given repentance. They repeated ancient history (Numbers 13-14). There is a renewal of repentance that all of us want to keep. There is nothing more wonderful than to know that the Holy Spirit is dealing with you, and that you are convicted, and that you can hear his voice, and your heart is not hardened, that you could be changed from glory to glory. But these Hebrew Christians would never know that again.

What did they lose?
So the first thing that the person described in Hebrews 6:6 cannot be renewed to is *repentance*. That is, the repentance that God grants and affirms. Caleb's opponents 'repented' (Numbers 14:40) but it was not what God put in their minds.

But to elaborate on what I mean by that, I would add, he or she cannot be renewed also to *enlightenment*. Someone will say, Can you give us a scripture for that? I can, and it is one of the most obscure, but plain passages in all the New Testament. How many of you know about 2 Peter 1:9? He has just said:

> Make every effort to add to your faith goodness; and to goodness, knowledge; and to knowledge, self-control; and to self-control, perseverance; and to perseverance, godliness; and to godliness, brotherly kindness; and to brotherly kindness, love. For if you possess these qualities in increasing measure, they will keep you from being ineffective and unproductive in your knowledge of our Lord Jesus Christ.

Now look at verse 9. How many of you have seen it? And thought about it? 'But if anyone does not have them'—we could say, if he lacks these qualities, he is not saved, he has not been converted. But that is *not* what Peter says. He says, 'if anyone does not have them, he is near-sighted and *blind*'. He cannot be renewed to enlightenment, for he is blind and cannot see far off, and has forgotten that he *was purged of his old sins.* He had been converted.

And then, according to the writer, another thing such cannot be renewed or brought back to, is *newness.* We often sing, Thy mercies are new, Great is thy faithfulness. What happens to a person who has been renewed, but whose senses are not exercised to discern good and evil, whose heart becomes hard, and who reaches the place where these actual Hebrew Christians were? A person loses the newness. There is nothing more thrilling to see than an older Christian who is still excited about the Lord. It is always fresh.

A person's *endowment*, their anointing, is also lost. Here is what I mean. Someone like this has been given an anointing, a certain ability, but if they do not use it, like the man who hid his talent, it will be taken away. A person who once had an unusual anointing finds that it has gone, and this is another way of saying that they cannot be brought back to. It will never be the same again.

Another thing is simply, *will*. People like this eventually have no will-power, no ability to control what they say, what they do.

Something else masters them. And that can happen, and I have seen people like this. They say, 'I know, I am in terrific bondage and there is nothing I can do about it.' There was a time when Christ was real to them, but they are in a bondage, with no will-power.

Also, *assurance*. A person like this becomes confused, and has little confidence. No presence of the mind of the Holy Spirit, no inner ease and rest of soul.

Last, but not least, a person is not *renewed to love*. People like this have no sense of forgiving another person; it just does not enter their minds. They have no capability along this line. They are likely to continue on and on in their vendetta—either to destroy others or to vindicate themselves.

They are blind and near-sighted, and have forgotten that they were actually purged from their old sins.

I said earlier that there are two ways that this is possible. There is the *particular* way this can be applied, and there is the *general*. Now by particular, what do I mean? Having been given a special calling, perhaps in a particular case, or at a particular time, you did not obey the Lord. Perhaps there was a chance for you to do something that God wanted you to do but you just did not, you blew it, and you can never get it back. Can you think of anything like that? I can recall situations in my own life where I just blew it, and what I might have been able to do for the Lord at a particular time and particular place, I lost, I cannot get it back. So there is a particular way that this can happen.

What about the general? Well the *general* means that there comes in the end a *life of uselessness*, where your usefulness has now been forfeited, and it is shipwrecked and this is what Paul himself feared (1 Cor. 9:27). So this is what did happen to those described in Hebrews 6.

Crucifying the Son of God all over again

The Greek literally reads, 'Those having fallen away to renew again unto repentance, re-crucifying to themselves the Son of God.' The word, *stauros*, meaning the cross, used as a verb means 'crucify', and this is a participle *(anastaurountas)* in the present tense, accusative masculine plural—Now, seeing that they crucify again. And any time you have the word, *ana*, in the Greek language, it means again, or like the hyphenated word 're', as re-crucified.

I will give you an illustration that you will probably recognise. Did you ever hear the expression 'Anabaptist'? Why were they called Anabaptists? Well, in the seventeenth century there were certain people in this country who believed that baptism, to be baptism, had to be upon profession of faith. I do not mean to get into controversy here, I am just stating an historical illustration of the prefix *ana*. So there were adults who, though having been baptised as a baby, decided that their infant baptism was not really baptism, and therefore they asked to be baptised. Those who were against this nicknamed them 'Anabaptists'; it was a pejorative term which said they 'rebaptised'.

We need to remember that it was our sin that crucified Jesus in the first place. 'All we like sheep have gone astray, and the Lord laid on him the iniquity of us all.' I do not think many reading this book will have much difficulty in believing that. What is it, then, to re-crucify him? It is to persist, wilfully, in the same sin of which you have been forgiven. This shows the inseparable connection between conversion and sanctification. When a person is converted, what is it that he is forgiven of? He is forgiven of his sins. The person who has been saved is commanded to leave his former ways.

Now, some preachers say, and I have said it myself, that when you become a Christian, you are forgiven all your sins, past, present, and future. And I believe that, insofar as it means that you will go to heaven. But do you know what Paul literally says? Romans 3:25, 'Whom God hath set forth to be a propitiation through faith in his blood, to declare his righteousness for the remission of sins that are *past*' (the Authorised Version has got it exactly right). What Paul meant is that when a person is converted, the *past* is washed away, and the assumption is that from then on he is going to serve the Lord and walk in the light.

John says, 'If we walk in the light, as he is in the light, we have fellowship with one another, and the blood of Jesus, his Son, purifies us from all sin' (1 John 1:7). But if we do *not* walk in the light, what does that mean? In Hebrews 10:26 we have a parallel warning: 'If we deliberately keep on sinning after we have received the knowledge of the truth, no sacrifice for sins is left.' So here is a person who had been converted, who knew that his or her sins were washed away, the past forgiven, who began to walk with the Lord, but at some stage lapsed, and returned to the sin of which he or she was originally forgiven. You say, surely not? Well, there have been Christians that did so. And should the person return to the sins of which they have been forgiven, although they do not lose their eternal salvation, there are serious consequences nonetheless. And it is to this the writer refers.

Here is further proof that the writer is not speaking of the blasphemy against the Holy Spirit. This sin, according to Mark, is committed by someone who refuses to acknowledge who Jesus is. 'Jesus said, "I tell you the truth, all the sins and blasphemies of men will be forgiven them. But whoever blasphemes against the Holy Spirit will never be forgiven; he is guilty of an eternal sin." He said this because they were saying, "He has an evil spirit"' (Mark 3:28-30). Now the blasphemy of the Holy Spirit has to do with denying that Jesus is the Son of God; Paul said, 'No man can say that Jesus is Lord but by the Holy Spirit,' and also, 'No-one who is speaking by the Spirit of God says "Jesus be cursed".' So what the writer of Hebrews is doing is referring to those people who *knew* who Jesus was, that he had died on the cross for them, and they *acknowledged* that he was the Son of God.

Now, people who deny that Jesus is the Son of God have no forgiveness, neither in this world, nor in the world to come. So that those who fell aside, in Hebrews 6, knew who Jesus was, he was the Son of God. If they had not been forgiven once, there could be no basis for a *re-crucifixion* of the Son of God, for there is no point in the writer using this word 're-crucify'. Here is another implication that he is talking about saved people. Since he says re-crucify, it is similar to having the word 'renewed again'. Their past sins were atoned for, but apparently these in Hebrews 6 turned back to their sins, and persisted in them.

The effectiveness of the gospel

When Jesus said, 'All the sins and blasphemies of men will be forgiven them', he right then and there said that he had something better to offer than the Aaronic priesthood. If you remember, the priesthood of Aaron could not atone for sin that was presumptuous (Numbers 15:30); there must therefore be something better than the priesthood of Aaron because it would not have atoned, for instance, for David's sin. This very theological rationale has been used by commentators to say that Hebrews 6 can only refer to presumptuous sin that was worthy of going 'outside the camp' and therefore these people were not covered by the blood of sacrifice.

When I read this, I could not believe it. I wanted to say, 'Are you telling me that the blood of Jesus Christ is limited to a certain kind of sin?' The Hebrew word translated to describe the kind of sin that was not covered by the priesthood of Aaron is usually *iniquity*. It was the worst kind of wickedness, and that kind of wickedness was not covered by the Levitical atonement. But what do we learn from this letter to the Hebrews? Their sins and *iniquity*, God will remember no more. The Lord has laid on Jesus the iniquity of us all. Only Christ's atonement could cover the kind of sinning of which David had been guilty.

When the writer says, 'crucify to themselves', he is saying that they will bear the brunt of their own sins. Uncleansed sin has serious consequences in this life. At the judgment seat of Christ they will be saved by fire. There will be no reward, their own sins shall haunt them, but they will be saved, because the Lord laid on Jesus the iniquity of us all.

What a pity if the gospel we preach is only going to atone for the sins that are not too bad! That is as far as the Levitical provision went (Heb. 5:2). But the gospel gives hope that those who put their trust in Jesus have assurance that *all* sin is forgiven. But the analogy is, in the same way that those outside the camp could *not* have their sins atoned for, so presumptuous sin in the Christian means he *cannot* have within himself the assurance of sin cleansed. There is, therefore, the implication of having no sense of repentance or enlightenment or usefulness in this life. So the analogy is there, between the children of Israel and those who were outside the camp, and the way a Christian is to live now.

The sin which hurts the cause of Jesus Christ is the equivalent of being put outside the camp in the Old Testament. The Greek word here is probably the longest Greek word I have ever seen— *paradeigmatizontas*, the present participle, which means 'to make an example of', or 'bring into shame'. This is precisely what the man in Corinth had done. For Paul said, 'There is sexual immorality among you, and of a kind that does not occur even among pagans'. And that did bring Jesus Christ's name into open shame, for here was a man who claimed to be saved, and he was living with his step-mother. It was a scandal, so the apostle Paul said, 'Get him out! Deliver him to Satan!' It was the equivalent of being put outside the camp, excommunication. But never once did Paul say that the problem with the man was that he had never been converted. Paul said, 'Deliver him unto Satan that his spirit may be saved on the day of the Lord.' The man, as I mentioned in the previous chapter, did repent, and Paul said, 'Bring him back.' So he was renewed, but presumably had he *not* repented, then he too would fall into the category of those described in Hebrews 6:6.

13

Put Christ To An Open Shame

They are crucifying the Son of God all over again and subjecting him to public disgrace (Hebrews 6:6c).

Many a minister has had to be a Nathan to a particular person who has fallen into sin. Such a one tries to help with Galatians 6:1 in mind: 'Brothers, if someone is caught in a sin, you who are spiritual should restore him gently. But watch yourself, or you also may be tempted.' I know what it is to go up to somebody who has fallen. Sometimes it is an encouraging experience. I put my arm around them and say, 'I am sorry. I understand. It can happen to me too.' It is wonderful when a person takes it in the right spirit and says, 'Thank you for coming to me like this.' We just pray together and say, 'Let's forget it, let's go on.' But then I know what it is like to go to somebody who will have the opposite reaction; there is recalcitrance, rebellion and hostility.

What happens then to people like this? I think we could put it like this: first of all, they forfeit usefulness; second, they forfeit fellowship with the Father; and third, they forfeit any kind of a reward in heaven, unless they are restored.

The particular point that the writer of Hebrews makes is that those described in Hebrews 6:4-6 cannot be renewed any more to repentance, which is the thing that is commensurate with fellowship with the Father. If after grieving the Lord, he deals with us, we can immediately say, 'Ah, I am sorry! God forgive me!', the fellowship with him is virtually unbroken. But when a person becomes hard, then they do not hear the voice of God as they used to do. And so we read in Numbers 14:20, 'The Lord replied, "I have forgiven them, as you asked."' So the children of Israel were *forgiven*, and you may differ with me on this (I am not in a position to say that every one of them was saved), but I think generally speaking, the point that Paul makes in 1 Corinthians 10 is that these people were a forgiven people, but they would not in their lifetimes enter Canaan. This is another reason I believe that Hebrews 6:8 is describing those who have been saved, and who will be in heaven but saved only as by fire: 'whose end is to be burned.'

Now a further indication of all this is we are told they crucified Jesus a second time. The first time Jesus was crucified was for the sins of the world, and the only way he could be re-crucified would be that those who had been forgiven would turn right back into that same sin. There must have been the acceptance of the forgiveness offered by his shed blood the first time, in order for there to be this expression, re-crucified. And so the way one can re-crucify the Lord is to fall right back into and persist in the very sins for which one was forgiven.

Put him to an open shame

This could not possibly refer to people in the world, for those who have never trusted Christ as Saviour cannot put him to open shame. We talk to people about the Lord, and they may laugh at us. One man on a Saturday in front of our church said to me, 'I am going to get the police to come and deal with you', and I hoped he would as then I could get to witness to that particular policeman. But although that man was so unpleasant, he was not putting the name of Christ into open shame. He could have blasphemed if he had wanted to, but he would not have brought the name of Christ into open shame.

What we are talking about then, are those who have been saved, who have received forgiveness. We are dealing with the same kind of thing for which the Old Testament priesthood could not atone. The Greek word for 'open shame' is very difficult to translate. It has the idea of making an example or putting one into contempt, as if I were to embarrass somebody, make an example of them. Jesus died for our sins and when we accept the forgiveness of sins, it is assumed that we turn from them and walk with the Lord. But when one goes back (and it does happen), then the name of Christ is brought to a place where it is a scandal; like embarrassing someone, it embarrasses the Lord, that is the plainest way to put it.

The worst thing that can happen would be if the *world* sees it take place. It is bad enough if it is just known in the church; it makes everybody feel uneasy and it is an unhappy situation. But let the world find it out, and they find it something to reproach the church for. This had apparently happened to the Hebrew Christians, for they had come to the place that the writer said they could not be renewed again unto repentance.

Hopefully you can see an analogy between the Old Testament priesthood and Hebrews 6:6. The Levitical priesthood did not cover sins that were scandalous. There was no atonement for those who sinned with a high hand, who were guilty of presumptuous sin. There *needed* to be a way that people like that *could* be saved; and that is partly why there had to be a priest after the order of Melchizedek. This shows the deficiency of the Old Testament priesthood to which some of the Hebrew Christians were tempted to return. But Jesus can save *all* manner of sins and blasphemies among men. The point is, although genuinely converted Christian people can do strange things, one should not say that there is no hope for them, because Christ's atonement gives hope for anybody.

What came within the scope of Old Testament sacrifice is similar to what comes within the potential scope of usefulness, fellowship with the Father, and a reward. This is the way God wants his people to be. Believers sin through ignorance, we have errors where we slip up. We all sin every day, but not with a high hand. So if we can keep in mind as long as one's sins come within the scope of non-scandalous sins (if I may put it that way and not be misunderstood), then one may have hope that he or she will not forfeit their usefulness, will not forfeit fellowship with the Father, and will not forfeit the reward in heaven.

Yet I have to say more. Even the absence of a scandal is no

guarantee that one will enter into God's rest. It is possible simply
to live a life that is beyond reproach, respectable, upstanding,
and still come short of the rest that remains for the people of God.
The reason I know this to be true is that the writer himself says
when he earlier brought up the subject of Melchizedek, 'I have
got many things to say about him, but you could not handle it
because you are so dull of hearing.' The writer knew that these
very Christians, though their lives had not brought the name of
Christ into reproach, still lacked something. They were not
enjoying this rest that the writer is putting before them in the
letter. You may feel that you have not done anything that would
bring the name of Christ into ill repute, or open shame and
reproach. But I tell you this: if someone *stays* in a dull, sluggish
condition, they most certainly will not enter into God's rest. Yet
the writer says, 'We are confident of better things in your case—
things that accompany salvation.' The warning, therefore, was
needed for them.

I wonder if I could put it in still another way. I do not know
whether this is a category that is a safe one always to hold to, but
let me just say that there probably are basically two kinds of sins:
voluntary and involuntary. I will try to explain what I mean. In
Hebrews 10:26 when the writer comes back to this same kind of
warning, he says, 'If we deliberately keep on sinning after we
have received the knowledge of the truth, no sacrifice for sins is
left.' This is the same thing as sinning with a high hand:
presumptuous sin, which is what David did with Bathsheba. Yet
the very way the text is worded implies there is sin that could be
described as voluntary.

What about involuntary sin?
This could be misunderstood and this is why I put this category
somewhat guardedly, because I would not want to imply that
people, when they sin, are unconscious of what they are doing.
There is a sense in which any sin is voluntary, as James says in
his letter, 'We all stumble in many ways' (3:2). This is
encouraging when you realise that James, the brother of our

Lord, was just about to write about the tongue, 'if anyone is never at fault in what he says, he is a perfect man', and he introduces it by saying, 'I am not perfect because we all stumble in many ways'. So there is a sense in which sin is involuntary, because before we know it we have said something we should not have said. Every day or two, I think of something I should not have said. But we all offend. So that is what I mean by involuntary sin.

Could I put it this way? We could categorise sin as scandalous and non-scandalous. Maybe you could describe it better, but for now I would put this before you as a way of understanding. Sin with a high hand in the Old Testament brought David to a place where his enemies could laugh at him: 'by doing this you have made the enemies of the Lord to show utter contempt' (2 Sam. 12:14). God cares about his own reputation, so in the same way, the name of the church in a community is very important. He is a jealous God.

A list of dangers
Now I will say what I would describe as a pastoral clue. I want to end this chapter in a way that you will apply it to your lives. I will give a list of the kind of things we need to be aware of, to know whether we might be in any danger of coming into the category of Hebrews 6.

The first I would put is this: *scandalous deportment*. In other words, how you carry yourself before people. Whenever there is a scandalous deportment, where there is a carelessness in the way you live, that is something to be very careful about indeed.

Secondly, I would list *harmful influence*. Somebody once asked me a question, Is it possible to lead another Christian astray and cause them to lose their reward? In Romans 14 is the way the apostle Paul put it, 'If your brother is distressed because of what you eat, you are no longer acting in love. Do not by your eating destroy your brother for whom Christ died.' 'Destroy' does not mean that he loses his salvation, but he is so crushed that his spirit is broken. It is possible that you can lead another astray by what you say to them, by what you say to somebody about another person. I do not know of anything sadder than this, when there are Christians in the congregation who will say something to a younger Christian that influences them in such a way that from that moment on, they lose a certain edge in their spiritual lives. Perhaps they thought the preacher was fine, they were just enjoying themselves, and then somebody comes up and says something against the minister, or against one of the deacons, and the person is never quite the same again. An innocent person, having heard this report, just is not the same again, and he or she is destroyed. Their sense of usefulness is gone. This is what I mean, in part, by harmful influence.

Thirdly, I would put down here in the list of dangers, *antagonism to the Spirit*. If when the Holy Spirit begins to deal with you, and show you things, you are hostile, then this is a very precarious state to be in.

Fourthly, I would mention *militant in grudges*. Jesus said, 'If you do not forgive men their sins, your Father will not forgive your sins' (Matt. 6:15). I think people who develop a habit of not forgiving those who have harmed them, become sluggish in their own spirituality, and dull of hearing, so that they reach the point when any message about love and offering total forgiveness has no impact at all. They cannot be renewed to repentance if their hearts remain cold and hard.

My fifth feature is *entrenchment in revenge*. This is one who is determined to get revenge over what anybody has done to him or her. Maybe you have been hurt, maybe somebody has let you down, maybe you have been lied about, maybe somebody has stomped on you and treated you like dirt, and the only thing you can live for is the day you get even. Let me tell you right now, you are the impoverished one, and you had better remember God says, 'It is mine to avenge; I will repay'.

The next thing we should beware of I would describe as *fraudulent in affairs*. This applies to those in business. How do you treat customers? What about your honesty, your reputation? What if you are known to be a Christian and it turns out that you are cutting corners or whatever? A certain amount of that may be legitimate business if you are wanting to save money, but any time you do not tell the truth, any time you mislead, this is a way of bringing the Lord's name into open scandal.

The seventh is *unrepentant when chastened*. When God chastens you, what is your reaction to it? There are three kinds of chastening: internal, that is when the Holy Spirit deals with you through the preached word; external, that is when God sends a Nathan the prophet to scold you; and there is terminal chastening, that is at the judgment seat of Christ. It is important that we recognise when God is chastising us, whether through preaching, through Bible study, or whatever. Are you going to be unrepentant in your chastening? If so, it will lead to the kind of situation that we have in Hebrews 6. I believe that had not David responded well to Nathan he too would have been in a Hebrews 6:6 situation.

The last thing is *lukewarm in enthusiasm*. Jesus said to the church of the Laodiceans, 'So, because you are lukewarm— neither hot nor cold—I am about to spit you out of my mouth' (Rev. 3:16). If you just sort of *remain* on the fence, and you vacillate back and forth, whether to go on with God or not, there is only a lukewarmness there. You are not cold, you are most certainly not on fire. Lukewarm. That, with all of these other things, is a borderline kind of Christian living, and can, if not dealt with, bring one to the place where God just says, 'I declared on oath in my anger, They shall never enter my rest.' You forfeit your inheritance, you forfeit the reward, and from then on you are of no use as long as you live.

14

Fruit

Land that drinks in the rain often falling on it and that produces a crop useful to those for whom it is farmed receives the blessing of God. But land that produces thorns and thistles is worthless and is in danger of being cursed (Hebrews 6:7-8a).

I do not like controversy, especially when it appears that I am contradicting certain aspects of traditional Reformed teaching. I regard myself as Reformed, even if I depart from the traditional Reformed position at certain points.[1] And we need to keep in mind whenever we get exercised about the finer points, that there is more which we have in common with the traditional Reformed teaching, than what we differ on. We must never forget that, and I long for the day when all suspicions will subside.

My view, none the less, of this passage, as I have stated several times in this book, is this: that the writer addresses in this section saved people, people whom we shall see in heaven. This is despite him having said, 'though by this time you ought to be teachers, you need someone to teach you the elementary truths of God's word all over again' (Heb. 5:12). Despite that, he believes they are saved, and indeed, he believes not only that they are saved, but they are going to be described among those who have fruit, things that *accompany* salvation (v. 9). In addition, those that he is speaking about in verses 4-6 are saved, otherwise why give descriptions of them that describe saved people everywhere else in the Bible. I say they are saved, for what more could saved people want than to have these things said about them?

---

1. Some readers may be puzzled by this word, Reformed. It largely refers to what is called Calvinism—the teaching of John Calvin (1509-1564) and his followers, not all of whom followed him at every point.

The salvation of such people is not in question, but what is in question is whether there is that which *accompanies* salvation. So he says, in verse 9, 'dear friends, we are confident of better things in your case—things that *accompany* salvation.' What is it he believes will *accompany* salvation? In a word, *lasting fruit*. What if there is no lasting fruit? The answer is, there will be a burning—'In the end it will be burned' (v. 8) and there will be loss of reward. They shall be saved but they shall suffer loss (1 Cor. 3:15).

The parable of the sower

What we will need to do in this chapter is to look at the Parable of the Sower and of what Jesus taught about the Vine and the branches in John 15, because there are certain things in this passage which remind us of both these sections. When we compare the Parable of the Sower with this passage, we can see why they are similar. But when we get really close, and look at them side by side, I think we will see that it does not fit at every point.

The Parable of the Sower (Matt. 13; Mark 4; Luke 8) refers to the initial response of people to the gospel itself; it shows the way in which seed was sown. Jesus said the seed is the word of God. So we must remember that the Parable of the Sower describes the way it was sown, how some initially responded when the word of God was sown; Hebrews 6:7-8 refers to our continued response to both the word and the Spirit.

So Hebrews 6:7-8 refers to those in whom the word of God has already been sown, they have already responded affirmatively to the gospel, but there are two kinds of continued response to the word and to the Holy Spirit, symbolised here as falling rain:

> *Land* that *drinks in the rain often falling* on it and that produces a crop useful to those for whom it is farmed receives the blessing of God. But *land* that *produces thorns and thistles* is worthless and is in danger of being cursed. In the end it will be burned.

The second kind of response to the word and Spirit (a negative response, alas) is obviously verse 8. The NIV even inserts the word 'land'; it is not in the Greek but it is implied, and there is nothing really wrong in doing so. What the writer does is to summarise this difficult section by a simple analogy. It is an illustration from nature: land that soaks up rain. He is saying what we all know, that sometimes the land produces a crop; other times the land produces thorns and briers. The vegetation or crop receives blessing from God, but that land which produced thorns, thistles, briers, is rejected or useless; it will be cursed and its end is to be burned.

In verse 7 we hear about blessing from God; in verse 8 cursing from God. Now the key to understanding this passage is this word, *usefulness*. In fact the Authorised Version took the liberty of translating *adokimos*, in verse 8, as 'rejected'. *Dokimos* is a word that means approved, but whenever you have a little 'a' in front of it (it is called the alpha privative), it means just the opposite. Dis-approve. It is exactly the same word used in 1 Corinthians 9:27 but translated in the Authorised Version as 'castaway' and in the NIV as 'disqualified'. I could more easily have chosen 1 Corinthians 9 as the parallel passage to Hebrews 6:7-8.

There have been those who believe one can lose his salvation and they base that partly on 1 Corinthians 9:27. In the same way others who believe a person can lose his salvation appeal to Hebrews 6:8. It is the same word in both places, and the same thing is discussed in both places. For what Paul feared in 1 Corinthians 9 was losing his reward or prize. He knew he was saved, Paul did not have any question about his own salvation. He said, 'I know whom I have believed, and am convinced that he is able to guard what I have entrusted to him for that day' (2 Tim. 1:12). Paul was not worried about his own salvation, but he knew that there was a real possibility that he might not gain the prize.

If Paul could say that about himself, it is certainly true of me, and I believe it is true of you. Our response to the rain, the showers of the Holy Spirit faithfully falling on us, will determine whether there is lasting fruit that will accompany salvation. This is why we must keep warm hearts that hear his voice. If we become cold, defensive and entrenched rather than being open and soaking in the rain of the Spirit, we are in danger of never being used again. The more you see of your own heart, and realise your own capabilities, then you will believe that it is possible that you could lose your reward. Just before Paul was going to be martyred by Caesar, he wrote in his last letter, 'The time of my departure is at hand.' But Paul was prepared now to say, 'Now there is in store for me the crown of righteousness' (2 Tim. 4:8). He knew then that nothing was going to happen in the next day or two to cause him to lose his reward. But when he wrote to the Corinthians he had years left, and would not make that statement.

I believe that is the key to understanding this passage. We need to keep the whole perspective of the writer in mind. In verse 7, he is talking about an illustration from nature, and everybody knows there is one kind of farming that produces fruit, and another that does not. If it does not produce fruit, if it grows nothing but thistles and briars, what is it good for? It is good for nothing. As Jesus said, in John 15, 'It is cut down and cast into the fire.' The writer to Hebrews says, 'whose end is to be burned.' We do not know for sure that our writer, whoever he was, knew about John 15, but we can see that there is a connection.

There are two more things that suggest to me a connection with the parable of the Sower. The first is that Jesus said, when giving the account, The word of God fell among thorns. This is the same word that is used here in verse 8. And yet, it is not quite the same, because the difference between the Parable of the Sower and Hebrews 6:8 is that in the Parable of the Sower, the word fell among thorns that were already growing up, whereas Hebrews 6:8 talks about land which produced thorns.

The second thing is, in the Parable of the Sower, some seed fell on good ground; the very fact that Jesus could say good ground implies there is ground that is not good. And we know that is true because if you can imagine a little path, and the sower is walking down the path, some of the seed will fall on the path, where there is no depth of earth, and it cannot grow. Or there might be some ground that is rocky and that is not good ground. And there is some ground where there are thorns, that is not good ground.

What the parable of the Sower does not imply is that these initial professions of faith could never be otherwise. In other words, if you want to take the parable of the Sower which describes the way the word of God is preached and the way it is received, and attach it to Hebrews 6, then you are bound to be consistent and say that those where the seed fell on the path, stony ground or whatever, could *never* have another chance. I know of no-one who believes that!

Let me give an illustration: I am sure that evangelism in the New Testament way is to have all four pictures taking place. We have those where the seed falls right on the path and there is no depth of earth; we have those where it falls on rocky ground— no soil, no moisture and so forth; we have sowing among thorns; and we have the good ground. I made an observation to a friend of mine that the ideal church situation is where you have all four taking place all the time: where you have got some where you know they have not been saved; others you are not sure whether they are or not, they start out with a great joy and then three months later you do not see them; yet others start out with the Lord and then something happens, they get discouraged, persecuted; and then you have those that just grow. I think the problem with many churches today, on both sides of the Atlantic, is that they think the only healthy church is where there is nothing happening but the falling on the good ground. They only want those who are going to persevere.

But a growing church surely is where we have all four types! Jesus presupposed that it would be a healthy church, that the parable of the Sower would be *needed*. I know churches where you do not need the parable of the Sower. What is so wonderful,

I believe, is when we are seeing it all. We ourselves have a lot who initially profess; we suspect they are not saved, but Jesus said, Expect that. And it is an unhealthy church where you do not see that. But are we going to say that these people who do suddenly fall away, and we do not see them coming back, are we going to say that they cannot be dealt with six months later? Are we prepared to say that, as Hebrews 6 says, *they* fell away and cannot be renewed again? I do not believe that at all! And that is another reason you cannot bring the Parable of the Sower into Hebrews 6 and make it fit every point.

There is no implication that I can see that the ground which produced thorns and briers is the same as we have in the third example of the parable of the Sower. For all I know those described in Hebrews 6:4-6, who had fallen away, had even professed a faith that once led them to thirty, sixty, and a hundred-fold fruit-bearing. In my heart of hearts, I believe those in Hebrews 6 are not only saved, but had excelled for a good while, some of whom had become stalwart saints. There is no other reason the writer would go into such detail. I think it can occur in an older Christian and when something happens, he stumbles and gets discouraged and *bitter*. I would not say for a minute that someone like that is not saved. I am not talking necessarily about falling into immorality, I am talking about a simple thing like two deacons falling out with each other, after both being Christians for years. When they get bitter, they just do not go to church any more, and I have seen some withdraw from the fellowship and get cold, and sometimes after warnings there is nothing further that can apparently be done to bring them back.

So we must not press the connection between the Parable of the Sower and Hebrews 6 too far. A closer connection, in my view, is John 15, if not 1 Corinthians 3 and 9.

John 15
The writer says, 'Land that drinks in the rain often falling on it.' Two things that can be said here. First, that the earth *drinks* in

rain. I believe the 'rain' refers also to the six graces described in
the earlier verses: repentance, illumination, tasting of the heavenly
gift, being made to share in the Holy Spirit, tasting the goodness
of God's word, and tasting the powers of the world to come.
Most certainly all saved people have these six graces showered
on them, but not all Christians apply the means of grace as they
should. So that is the first thing that is suggested by the writer's
analogy from nature.

The second is that a *good deal of time elapsed* before those
who fell away were judged to be unable to be renewed again unto
repentance. The writer says, 'Land that drinks in the rain *often*
falling on it'. Despite the fact that the rain came down and down
and down, and I doubt not that included warning after warning,
there was time involved. So that the falling away was not simply
in the same case of the seed that fell by the wayside and so forth.
Then he says that the land produces a crop, brings forth vegetation.
The Greek word is *botanen*, from which we get the word,
botany. It is the only time it is used in the New Testament but it
means 'vegetation, crop'. Obviously it refers to what Jesus
meant by fruit. This is why we can not unfairly bring in John 15.
For what Jesus called 'fruit' the writer in Hebrews 6 calls 'herb,
crop, vegetation'.

What can be said about fruit? It is vegetation that you can eat.
It is vegetation that nourishes. It can be seen, it can be felt. So
what the writer wants here is a crop that will be useful. Useful
to whom? For whom it is farmed. For those by whom it is cared
for. What we have here is that the crop is going to do something
for somebody else. But then there is one other aspect—had you
thought of this? What makes a crop, a crop? Does it just grow?
Although God does it, man has to till the soil, and take care of
it. The danger of these Hebrew Christians was that they had
become lazy, dull of hearing, slothful and so forth. What we
have here is an implicit indictment upon the laziness of those
Hebrew Christians.

Then he says that such a person receives blessing from God.
Now, why would he put it like that? It shows that God is going

to bless that which has already been produced. One thinks of the time when Jesus came and cursed the fig tree because there were no figs. And Jesus said, in John 15, I am the vine, my Father is the husbandman, and he said, Every branch in me must bear fruit. And so I ask, what is the blessing then, when he says that what produces a useful crop receives blessing from God?

I believe there are at least three ways in which this blessing can come. This is of course to say nothing of the blessing of being renewed to repentance and being useful!

Pruning
The first blessing is that it is pruned—being disciplined, or chastened: 'Every branch that does bear fruit he *trims clean* so that it will be even more fruitful' (John 15:2). So to the one where the fruit is produced, where you are useful, in your small way, I tell you this, if you are walking in the light, you are keeping a sweet spirit, not letting any bitterness come in: you submit to God's chastening, and you become aware that he deals with you, and you say, 'Yes, Lord, I will do what you say.' Whatever it is, he might tell you that he wants you to begin tithing, and you say, 'Lord, I will do it.' Whatever. It may be a small thing, it may be something big. Jesus said, 'He that is faithful in that which is least, is faithful also in much.' Now any time God gives you light on something, and you rebel, you become hostile, and you become entrenched and you spend the rest of your time proving that you were right, there is nothing but bitterness. There may be no further pruning!

A temporal reward
The second way this blessing can come is that there is a temporal reward. What do I mean by that? Well, God will give you knowledge, God will give you peace, God will give you influence, God will give you a convert. If you aspire to be a soul winner, you will eventually win a soul.

God *might* choose to bless you at the natural level. That he may prosper you I do not guarantee, but he just might, he does do that. It is true that you cannot outgive the Lord, but that is not an implicit promise of financial prosperity. It does not happen to everybody. I have been a tither for years and years and years, and I just live from week to week. Others are blessed in a material way, but I can tell you this, there is the promise of blessing from God if you walk in the light.

Eternal reward

What is the reward in heaven? I have to be honest and say that at this point in time I do not know. There are words like 'prize', 'crown', 'reward', which are probably symbolic—I do not know, I cannot say that you will not actually be given a crown. But I believe this, if you were to ask me right now what the reward is in heaven that Paul aspired to, it was simply to have the commendation of Jesus himself: 'Well done, well done.'

One of the first things I am going to look at are the twelve foundations of the New Jerusalem where the names of the apostles are engraved. I am interested to see who the twelfth apostle is, who it was that replaced Judas Iscariot. Will it be Matthias? Or will it be the apostle Paul? The very mention of their names suggests that God gave to them an eternal prestige, that they would live throughout eternity with the knowledge that they had pleased the Lord. That is the prize.

15

**The
Burning**

Land that drinks in the rain often falling on it
and that produces a crop useful to those for
whom it is farmed receives the blessing of God.
But land that produces thorns and thistles is
worthless and is in danger of being cursed. *In
the end it will be burned* (Hebrews 6:7-8).

We saw in the last chapter that there are two categories of
believers described in an allegorical way in verses 7 and 8. The
first category is a description of those who *do* go on to maturity
and the second refers to those who have been described as
having fallen away, so that they cannot be brought back to
repentance because they are crucifying the Son of God all over
again and subjecting him to public disgrace. Verse 8 corresponds
to people like that.

We also noticed the similarities and contrasts between these
verses and two other New Testament passages—the Parable of
the Sower and John 15. Another scripture which deals with
similar issues is 1 Corinthians 3:15, 'If it is burned up, he will
suffer loss; he himself will be saved, but only as one escaping
through the flames', and I want to look at that later in this
chapter.

In the previous chapter, I pointed out that the 'worthless'
referred to in verse 8 is the Greek word, *adokimos,* which is the
same word used in 1 Corinthians 9:27 by the apostle Paul where
it is translated 'castaway' in the Authorised Version and
'disqualified for the prize' in the New International Version. In
1 Corinthians 9:27, Paul clearly was not referring to the loss of
his own salvation; what he could lose was the reward, or prize.
I believe that this is what Hebrews 6:8 is equally referring to. I
put it like this: verse 7 refers to *blessing*, and verse 8 refers to
cursing.

In what way is one blessed?

If an individual goes on to maturity, goes on to perfection, how does the blessing come? Well, two ways that I will repeat: one is there will be a *pruning*, or a purging, because Jesus said in John 15, 'Every branch that does bear fruit he trims clean so that it will be even more fruitful.' It is like being changed from glory into glory, and maybe sometimes we feel that we have made great progress with the Lord, and we think, 'God is really blessing me and I must have arrived.'

But what God does is he prunes us, like gardeners cut the branches back. Often a person has been obedient to the Lord, yet suddenly he is chastened, for a part of the blessing is the pruning. But this is where God trims you. He cuts you back so as to bring more fruit. We are to remember that the Lord disciplines those he loves, and we never outgrow chastening in this life.

The other way is *reward*. I feel that God has rewarded me in this life again and again and again. But I think we need to keep mainly in mind our reward in heaven, in the future.

What about those who do not go on to maturity?

The answer is, cursing, or a rejection, or being unapproved, for actually the writer comes short of putting cursing here. He says 'in danger of being cursed'. What is that? It is God's judgment because there is no fruit.

What would be the consequences? The first is that there would be *no further spiritual development*. They cannot be renewed again unto repentance. The most important thing in your spiritual life is that there is a *daily* renewal of repentance— that your heart is sensitive to what grieves the Holy Spirit. You confess when you have erred; you admit it when you are wrong in your husband/wife relationship, or relationship in the college, or at work. You are quick to admit when you are wrong, that you are sensitive. Otherwise, you become entrenched. We have all run into people that never admit when they are wrong, who are always right. They just cannot apologise. Why is it? They have become *insensitive*, and they have no sense of repentance.

Deafness can happen at both a natural level and at a spiritual level. Regarding the latter, a person who just will not go on into maturity, and who takes the warnings of Scripture lightly, and who takes the doctrine of sanctification lightly, and takes holiness lightly, what happens is that they reach the place where they are hard of hearing and become stone-deaf, and there is going to be no further spiritual development.

The second consequence is *no reward*. And so in 1 Corinthians 3 we are told that one would suffer loss. 'If it is burned up, he will suffer loss; he himself will be saved, but only as one escaping through the flames.'

Now for that critical point that I mentioned here in verse 8: 'But land that produces thorns and thistles is worthless and is in danger of being cursed.' The word translated cursed is *katarus*, used six times in the New Testament; as far as I am able to tell, it always means doom, or condemnation, or cursing. 'As many as are under the law are under its curse.' 'Cursed is everyone that hangs on a tree.' It is talking about condemnation, doom, and there is no way out.

Three interpretations of 'cursed'

There are three interpretations of this verse that I know of.

One is from ancient times, the view of Chrysostom. He said, that it is a warning because there is still hope. He looked at this as an optimistic verse. The fact, said Chrysostom, that the writer said '*in danger* of being cursed' means that there is still hope. But most Bible scholars do not look at it that way.

Another way of interpreting it is that *in danger* or *nigh* (AV) means only a matter of time. Nigh unto cursing suggests that the cursing is inevitable.

The third way of looking at it is that the word, *in danger* or *nigh*, means coming perilously close to the same fate as those who are lost. It means near, not with regard to time, but with regard to *category*. The way it is interpreted by these scholars, is that the writer is simply saying these people who are rejected have become perilously close to those who were eternally lost.

I am inclined to the last view.

This word *cursed* is a strong word, and it seems only to be used to depict those for whom no hope whatever is held out. Therefore, I think we have got to say that those described in Hebrews 6:4-6 are irrevocably to be cursed; however if the *nigh* refers to time, they are inevitably lost and you must take the view that either they were not converted in the first place, or that the Arminians are right, they were saved but they lost their salvation. Some will no doubt want to take that position. But if you take the view that the nearness refers to that category who are very near to being cursed, it follows that because of the lives that they have lived, they are in danger of receiving that which those never saved will receive, namely, an eternal doom. But by God's sheer grace they don't receive it.

This was the thing about the man in Corinth, who was, as Paul said, guilty of a sin that does not occur even among pagans, it was disgraceful. It is always a disgraceful thing when a person who is known to be a Christian falls into sin. Yet we are told that the man in Corinth, and his fellow Christians, were puffed up about it. But Paul told them to hand him over to Satan, so that his spirit would be saved in the day of the Lord Jesus. And he was saved, but he was very near the category of those who are cursed.

Another example is that of Lot, Abraham's nephew, who foolishly lived in Sodom. We know that he was saved in the nick of time. Yet the Bible describes him as 'just Lot', referring obviously to the righteousness of Christ which was imputed to him.

We will have to decide whether we think the 'nigh' refers to time, or to category—whether it is inevitable they are going to be cursed, or whether that it is just that they are very close to the category that will be cursed. I have done a little study on the Greek, and I can tell you that it is used both ways, so we will not be able to resolve the problem by understanding the Greek. I can give you an example of each: Matthew 24:32, 'that the summer is near', refers to time; in Luke 19:11 Jesus is 'near Jerusalem', which refers to place, somewhere you are close to. The Greek can help you out many times but not always.

In the end it will be burned
The end of this verse reads 'in the end it will be burned'. The Authorised Version has a more literal translation—'whose end'—for the word translated 'whose' is the genitive feminine singular, and it is probably describing the cursing, which is also in the genitive singular. So there is no doubt what the writer is on to here. The final outcome of this category described in verse 8 is burning.

On this point I believe all scholars are agreed that the reason for the burning is obvious—thorns and briers are useless, they have no value, they are good for nothing, they are worthless. We are not talking therefore about people, we are talking about works. One would not want to say that an immortal soul is worthless. So what is worthless is not the person, but his works. For it is their works that prove these people have become useless.

It is interesting that scholars just do not want to deal with this. I do not know why; it is God's infallible word. I have twenty commentaries in my study on Hebrews, and I have been amazed how many scholars do not even want to comment on this phrase, 'In the end it will be burned.' A. W. Pink does not go into it; John Calvin does not; Donald Guthrie does not; Philip Edgecumbe Hughes does not deal with it; even John Owen, who never missed anything and would spend pages on a semi-colon, has very little to say and one derives the conclusion from John Owen that the burning is eternal punishment, eternal hell.

But I do not think we need to be in any mystery about it. We can turn to two other passages in the New Testament that sound very like the burning of Hebrews 6:8—John 15:6 and 1 Corinthians 3:15.

John 15:6 is preceded by the verse that says 'Every branch in me'—the branch is in Jesus—'He [the Father] cuts off every branch in me that bears no fruit.' The Arminians, of course, say that this proves someone can lose their salvation because it says 'in me'. But if a person is *in him*, obviously that person is saved. Therefore I would insist that the person does not lose salvation, but not having fruit renders that this branch is cast into the fire. It is not a reference to eternal punishment in hell, but to the same burning as Hebrews 6:8.

1 Corinthians 3:15 says the exact same thing: 'If it is burned up, he will suffer loss; he himself will be saved, but only as one escaping through the flames'. I have an illustration that may help us understand Paul's teaching. Take a metal tray and let it represent the foundation, in this case Jesus Christ. Put on the tray gold, silver, precious stones, wood, hay, stubble and mix them up together. Then pour over it some kerosene, throw a match on it, and it will go up in flames. Five minutes later, what will be there? It will be the gold, the silver, the precious stones.

It is a similar illustration that Paul uses here in 1 Corinthians 3:12: 'If any man builds on this foundation using gold, silver, costly stones, wood, hay or straw, his work will be shown for what it is...'. Every believer is going to be exposed, our work will be made manifest. You may think that you do not need to worry about that; you may say, 'I am covered by the blood of Christ, I do not need to worry!' But Paul further says that 'every man's work will be shown for what it is, because the Day will bring it to light. It will be revealed with fire, and the fire will test the quality of each man's work. If what he has built survives, he will receive his reward. If it is burned up, he will suffer loss; he himself will be saved, but only as one escaping through the flames.' That reads so clearly as to need almost no comment at all.

Let me close with this question, Is the fire literal? My honest answer is, I do not know, it may be figurative language. But the point is to show whether our good works are to be judged truly as good in God's sight. We are commanded to show good works.

Part Three

God's Encouragement Can Be Great

16

Hope For The Future!

Even though we speak like this, dear friends, we are confident of better things in your case—things that accompany salvation. God is not unjust; he will not forget your work and the love you have shown him as you have helped his people and continue to help them (Hebrews 6:9-10).

When the writer says, 'Dear friends, we are confident of better things in your case', he is obviously comparing the original readers of this Epistle to the Christians he has described in the previous verses. In this reference there are two sad descriptions. One is, some fell away so as to make a renewal again to repentance out of reach. The other thing said of them is that their end is to be burned—that which 'produces thorns and thistles is *worthless'* (verse 8), from the Greek word, *adokimos*, the same word which Paul uses in 1 Corinthians 9:27, when he feared that he himself might be a 'castaway'. Those who *are* so described are 'in danger of being cursed', whose end is to be burned. We have interpreted that to correspond to John 15:6 and 1 Corinthians 3, namely, that there will be those who will be saved as by fire, but in doing so, will lose a reward.

So when the writer says, 'we are confident of better things in your case', he is informing his readers that they have *not* yet reached that place where it is impossible for them to be renewed and where they could not ever have a reward.

Now why did he speak that way? For two reasons, a general and a particular. The general—because there was a universal principle at stake; the particular—because he knew something of the immediate situation in this Christian community.

The particular

As I have explained in previous chapters, the writer knew that there were those who *had* fallen away and could not be brought back to repentance. Obviously, they had been renewed before, or he would not have said, brought 'back', or 'renewed again'. This impossibility of renewal is not always the case. Jesus said to the church at Ephesus, 'Remember the height from which you have fallen! Repent...' (Rev. 2:5). The Galatian Christians had fallen, yet Paul said, 'I pray that Christ will be formed in you'.

Why is it that those referred to in Hebrews 6 cannot be restored? Because they had become stone-deaf. Spiritually speaking, this had set in for so long a time that they would never again be gripped by the Word of God. For such situations there is a definite principle. What is it? There comes a time when God simply gives up. It is similar to the children of Israel in the wilderness, when there came a time that God said, 'I declared on oath in my anger, they shall never enter my rest.' In 1 John 5 :16, mention is made of a sin that leads to death. This does not happen every day, but there are occasions when God acts in this way because the person will not repent.

It is a very delicate matter to know when to apply it. The writer was not only writing under inspiration, but using his pastoral expertise, if I may put it that way. I don't believe, in my own pastoral experience, that I've ever seen anybody that I would be prepared to say could not be renewed again to repentance.

Now, there is something very encouraging here for all of us. As long as we can sense the Holy Spirit dealing with us, we can be sure that we are *not* of those who cannot be renewed again. As long as we can hear when God speaks to us; or when we hear preaching and are convicted and smitten, we just say, 'Thank you, God, for your patience with me.'

These Hebrew Christians were themselves in a precarious state because the writer had said in chapter 5, 'You ought to be further along than you are, but you have become dull of hearing'—in other words, the condition of stone deafness could set in with them as well. This is why he does go into the general principle, because it is dangerous to reach the place where you don't hear the Word of God speaking to you. Yet the writer was confident of better things from them.

I go back to a pastoral care situation. People will come for spiritual help. Now, what principles will I be going by? Well, first of all, there is the general principle that I will be speaking from. But then there is the particular. I start talking to this person, based on the general principle, and I say, Well now, wait a minute, surely this is the case? But the general principle doesn't fit. The only way I can give help is if I get to know the person a bit. Sometimes in a few minutes, based on a conversation, I can make a judgment. I may not always be right—it requires great wisdom to be a pastor. And so here the writer, using his spiritual wisdom and applying a general principle, then comes to the particular when he says he is confident of better things *in their case*. And I trust in yours too!

Things that accompany salvation

Now, the things that accompany salvation would include the aforementioned blessing—but also crown, prize, reward. It also includes renewal of repentance! That of course is something that the apostle Paul wanted. In 1 Corinthians 9, the context is quite clear: Paul wanted the prize. And in a word, Hebrews 6:4-6 is describing those who, by falling away, could not be brought *back* to repentance, and so forfeited a reward. His readers had not yet reached the place that they could have no reward. So the emphasis is on the 'better things' that *accompany* salvation, namely, the inheritance of believers. Joseph Ton has said, 'Every child of God has an inheritance that rightfully belongs to him, but it is possible to lose it.' In my own life, I am still my grandmother's grandson although I lost my inheritance; I disappointed her. A person can write you out of their will, yet you are still their offspring. You are still in the family.

This is teaching which should motivate us. I don't know of any other teaching that will make us see how seriously the Bible takes this matter of rewards. But a lot of people just don't seem to take it too seriously. I believe this passage helps us to see that it is very important.

Some of the *things* that have persuaded the writer that his readers were still capable of being useful in God's service are mentioned in 10:32-34:

> Remember those earlier days after you had received the light, when you stood your ground in a great contest in the face of suffering. Sometimes you were publicly exposed to insult and persecution; at other times you stood side by side with those who were so treated. You sympathised with those in prison and joyfully accepted the confiscation of your property, because you knew that you yourselves had better and lasting possessions.

God will not forget your work

The writer says in 6:10: 'God is not unjust; he will not forget your *work* and the love you have shown him as you have helped his people and continue to help them.' That's a strange way to speak unless he is referring to something *other* than salvation.

This is a verse that some Roman Catholics use to prove being saved by works. Am I to believe that is the writer's theology? It most certainly is not. He doesn't say we are saved *because* of our works; he says, God is not unjust; he will not *forget* our work of love. The only way this fits in is if it has to do with renewal of repentance or with our reward. I don't mean to be disrespectful to any Roman Catholic who may be reading my book. I am merely teaching that we are saved by grace and yet God remembers our good works. What's the difference? That we know we are *saved* by the blood of Jesus Christ, and we are not *saved* by our works. But it is encouraging for me to know that God pays attention to me. He does notice me. Sometimes when I get discouraged, I think, Lord, it's not worth it; do I have to do this? Then I read a verse like this: God is not unjust to forget our work. The motivation is to know we are *saved* by grace, and yet that God also notices our work and labour of love.

Look at these verses:

And if anyone gives even a cup of cold water to one of these little ones because he is my disciple, I tell you the truth, he will certainly not lose his reward (Matt. 10:42).

Whatever you do, work at it with all your heart, as working for the Lord, not for men, since you know that you will receive [and look at the phrase] an *inheritance* from the Lord as a reward [there it is, the inheritance as a reward]. It is the Lord Christ you are serving. Anyone who does wrong will be repaid for his wrong, and there is no favouritism (Col. 3:23-25).

Your work will be rewarded (Jer. 31:16).

So as far as I am able to understand God's word, the only interpretation that makes sense (and it coheres with the whole of the New Testament) is that the writer is referring to things that *accompany* salvation, for example, rewards, not to mention the aforementioned six graces described in Hebrews 6:4-6. God is not unjust to forget your labour of love. These people are not saved because they minister to God's people. But because of their faithfulness, our conclusion is that good works carried out by those who were enlightened, tasted of the heavenly gift, shared in the Holy Spirit, tasted the good word of God and the powers of the world to come, *have an undoubted compensation*. What are they? Four things:

(1) God's justice takes their lives into account. He doesn't forget.

(2) Such people can be renewed again unto repentance, the same thing as being changed from glory to glory (2 Cor. 3:18).

(3) They will receive a reward at the judgment seat of Christ, if they continue as the writer believes they will.

(4) They are encouraged to believe that they may expect still greater things from God, and that is what the writer is leading up to, how Abraham obtained the promise after he patiently endured (Heb. 6:13-15).

So remember this, we are saved totally, wholly, categorically, absolutely, by grace. And yet what was it that God promised not to forget? Their work, their labour, and the love which they displayed to his name. The writer is saying, I don't believe that what has happened to those in verses 4-6 is going to happen to you. How could he make a judgment like that? Because he had noticed the love they had towards God.

Many of my congregation come in to see me because they fear they are described in Hebrews 6:4-6. I say to them, 'I'm not worried about you, not a bit! For I know the love you have for his name; I know your works.' Those who repeat the example of these described in Hebrews 6:4-6 never seek counsel as to whether they fit this pattern. They don't even know there is a problem.

17

Full Assurance

We want each of you to show this same diligence to the very end, in order to make your hope sure (Hebrews 6:11).

There are many expressions used to describe an advanced spiritual state: some call it the 'sealing of the Spirit', some call it 'the baptism with the Holy Spirit'; the writer of Hebrews has called it 'God's rest'. But now he is going to use a different expression: 'We want each of you to show this same diligence to the very end, in order to make your hope *sure.*'

This is a verse that gets right down to where we live. There is something here that is most precious. It is to see how easy it is for a person to get involved in things that are quite right and legitimate, but which do not help him spiritually.

Spiritual and practical

In this chapter I want to highlight both spiritual and practical aspects, and I will explain what I mean. On the spiritual side, the writer has already said, back in chapter 5:11 when he brought up the subject of Melchizedek, that these Hebrew Christians are dull of hearing. But he compliments them on the practical side in verse 10: God is not unjust; he will not forget your work and the love which you have shown him as you have helped his people and continue to help them.

How easy it is to confuse the spiritual and the practical! In Luke 10, we are told that Jesus visited the house of Martha and Mary. While he was talking there, Mary sat at Jesus' feet, but Martha had to fix the meal. Can you see what was going on? Having Jesus of Nazareth for a meal—wouldn't that be something? While Mary is talking to Jesus, Martha is in the

150

kitchen preparing the meal, and she is aware that her sister is talking to Jesus the whole time. I don't know how much time elapsed but she began to steam inside. Really, she is mad at her sister, but she is a bit annoyed at Jesus too because he should understand how she feels. So she comes in and she sort of rebukes Jesus. She says, 'Tell my sister she ought to help me with this meal!' But our Lord defends Mary: 'Martha, Martha, you are worried and upset about many things.'

It is similar in Hebrews 6:10 with these Jewish Christians. Though they were dull of hearing, they were most certainly not dull on the practical side. I mean, their labour of love was wonderful, and when it came to ministering to God's people, they were right there. So they were great doers in the sense of wanting to get things done on the practical side. Far better had they been like Mary! And yet the Marthas of this world also have hope!

I wonder if anyone reading this has thought, 'You've sure described me. When I was first converted, there was a zeal for the Lord, a sense of joy, his word meant so much to me, and there was a reality of his presence.' But at some stage, almost imperceptibly, the spiritual side gave in to the practical. And you thought, surely, this will be sufficient. Little things such as: giving a person a ride to church—a good thing to do; shopping for an elderly person; visiting the sick. These are all wonderful things. But what happens is that these activities, imperceptibly almost, begin to take the place of the spiritual. The spiritual side, what would this be? Personal prayer life; reading the Scriptures and taking the time to memorise them; witnessing; financial sacrifice; resisting temptation; keeping a warm heart. In short, walking in the light.

Therefore, when the writer says in verse 11, 'We want each of you to show this same diligence', he is referring to two actual features: first, how diligent they were at the practical level; second, the same zeal they had at the spiritual level, when they first were converted, needs to be restored. So here is the way I would like to put it. At the beginning they were known for their spirituality. How do we know that? In chapter 10:32-34, he says:

> Remember those earlier days after you had received the light,
> when you stood your ground in a great contest in the face of
> suffering. Sometimes you were publicly exposed to insult and
> persecution; at other times you stood side by side with those
> who were so treated. You sympathised with those in prison and
> joyfully accepted the confiscation of your property, because
> you knew that you yourselves had better and lasting possessions.

These Hebrew Christians, at one time, were spiritually very
sharp and there was nothing that could be said against them. But
at the time when the writer was addressing them, their current
problem was that they had begun to emphasise the practical side
almost exclusively, and had neglected the spiritual side. So
when the writer says, 'We want each of you to show the same
diligence', what he wants, first of all, is for them to put the same
diligence they have had at the practical level, into the spiritual
side. But also, by the same diligence he means that they could
recover what they had at the beginning.

We see from this a very interesting connection between the
practical and the spiritual. They are connected, yes, but they are
not the same. Both are noticed by God, but only one of them
leads to full assurance. That's the connection.

I have come up here with a little formula. Those of you who
major in physics and algebra, don't laugh at this, but ordinary
people can handle this one: PC + OZ = FA. Practical Concern
plus Original Zeal (you had when first converted) equals Full
Assurance. And this is the writer's point.

Here were these Hebrew Christians with something lacking
in them—but the objective assurance that they needed would
come only by concentrating on the spiritual. This is why Jesus
came to Mary's defence. It is a warning to all of us. Even those
at Bible College, who spend their time in Bible studies can, in
their souls, shrivel up. It is possible for you to do the tea, or work
in the book room, or work in the office, or whatever you do in
helping people, and not be any closer to God. God notices it, but
in order to come into this full assurance, this sure hope, you have
to show the same diligence in spiritual things.

Full assurance of hope

The way the writer approaches this is to go from the general to the particular. In verses 9 and 10, it is a general comment when he says, 'Dear friends, we are confident of better things in your case'. But in verse 11, he goes to the particular: 'We want each of you to show *this* same diligence.' The reason he puts it like that is because it would be wrong for some to assume that just because they are not in the category of those in verses 4 and 5, they are automatically going to reach the goal that he envisages. You might say, 'Thank God I am not in Hebrews 6:4-6.' But the fact that you're *not* in that category doesn't mean that automatically you *will* spiritually develop.

Show is a Greek word that literally means to give outward proof of. It is used in 2 Corinthians 8:24 for example, where the apostle Paul says: 'Therefore show these men the proof of your love and the reason for our pride in you, so that the churches can see it.' In 2 Timothy 4:14 it is simply translated by the little word *did*, when Paul says that Alexander the coppersmith 'did' me much evil.

The point is that we show it not merely with words or with the desire. What that means is that if the Holy Spirit is talking to you right now, you will feel the need to emphasise the spiritual. But it is not enough that you simply say, 'Well, I want to do something about it.' How often in a church service a person will be inspired and he will bow his head and worship and make promises to the Lord. But that's not *showing* it. You will never grow spiritually until you begin to *do* at the spiritual level. For example you can show the same diligence on Monday morning by setting your alarm clock thirty minutes earlier to have time with God in prayer. You *show* it.

Some Christians talk about knowing God, about having Jesus to be real to them, to be filled with the Spirit. Others may say, 'This has never happened to me.' Well, maybe why it hasn't happened to you is because you don't show the same diligence; you feel things, but nothing really grips you to the extent that you spend more time in prayer. I mean, how many minutes a day *are* you on your knees? How much are you reading your Bible? How many chapters do you read a day? I have heard many people say, 'I just can't keep up with the McCheyne Bible Reading Plan.' But you could. It depends on how much you want to be with Jesus. Mary wanted to be right there with him.

What's the goal then? Well here it is: a sure hope, or 'full assurance of hope' (AV). It is the Greek word *plerophoria* used four times in the Bible. In Colossians 2:2 it is translated 'full riches of understanding'. It comes twice in Hebrews, here and in 10:22 'full assurance of faith'. Paul also uses the same word to address the Thessalonians, when he says, our preaching came to you 'with deep conviction'. So *plerophoria* can apply to preaching with power and conviction.

Two kinds of assurance
When the writer refers to coming into full assurance, he emphasises the word *full*. This implies that they already had some assurance. At this point I am happy to say I am in delightful agreement with the historic confession of faith that says, 'This infallible assurance does not belong to the essence of faith.' It does not say assurance doesn't belong to the essence of faith, it says, *infallible* assurance does not belong to the essence of faith. There is a difference, because there is an element of assurance in faith. Because Jesus died on the cross for our sins, we know that if we trust in him we will go to heaven. That is assurance. The writer is not questioning whether his readers had that type of assurance, but whether they had come to the full or sure assurance of hope.

What exactly does he mean? He is pointing to an undoubted realisation of where you stand with God, not only with regard to your eternal destiny, but whether Jesus is spiritually real to you. The wonderful thing is that we are thinking about a possibility that *does* exist!

Now it may come gradually, or it may come suddenly. Some come into this suddenly and when they do they tend to think that those who haven't come into it suddenly don't have the real thing. There are those who have known since their conversion a remarkable instantaneous experience with God. Maybe it has happened with some of you. But it would be a mistake for you to say, Well, if it hasn't happened that way with others, then they don't know anything about this.

Let's take conversion itself. There are some people who know the day and the hour of their conversion, and there are others who really cannot tell you when it happened. Does that mean they are not saved? I often quote Toplady's famous statement: 'You may know the sun is up, although you were not awake the moment it arose'. So with this full assurance of hope. To some it can be sudden; to others it is gradual.

The point is the writer is telling us what to do about it: show the same diligence *to the very end*, in order to make your hope sure.

Lifetime commitment

Why does he talk about 'end'? For this reason—our diligence is to become a lifetime commitment unto death, right to the end. What happens is that when it does become a lifetime commitment, along the way you find that you *have* come into this full assurance of hope *before* the end.

Let me put it to you another way. Whenever you take upon yourself a commitment that is based upon a general spiritual principle, don't ever make the mistake of saying, 'Oh, I'll try it for a while.' Here's the person who gets convicted that tithing is right. But after two weeks there aren't any financial results, so he says, 'Oh, I don't think God wants me to tithe.' The point is that anything that is right—prayer, reading your Bible, resisting temptation—you don't do it because you get some great blessing or thrill out of it. It is a lifetime commitment. But, before the end, you *will* know this full assurance.

18

**How To Enter
The Big League**

We want each of you to show this same diligence to the very end, in order to make your hope sure. We do not want you to become lazy, but to imitate those who through faith and patience inherit what has been promised (Hebrews 6:11-12).

Now, as I said, there is more than one term or phrase for what the writer of Hebrews means by 'full assurance' or the sure hope. Elsewhere in this same letter, as we have seen already, he calls it 'God's rest'; in 10:35 it is referred to as a rich reward, when he says, 'Do not throw away your confidence; it will be richly rewarded'. It is called in Hebrews 12:11, 'a harvest of righteousness and peace'.

Paul also had more than one expression for it. The most beautiful of all, perhaps, is the way he put it to the Galatians. The Christians there had gone off the rails because they had decided that they would improve on God's way and so became enamoured with the law because they thought by doing it, they would be brought closer to God. But it turned out, Paul says, they had 'fallen from grace'. However, in praying for them, Paul asks that Christ will be *formed* in them—the same thing that we are talking about here.

Elsewhere Paul refers to full assurance like this: 'Having believed, you were marked in him with a seal, the promised Holy Spirit' (Eph. 1:13); and in Philippians 4:7 and Colossians 3:15, Paul calls full assurance the 'peace of God'. With regard to peace, biblical scholars have made a distinction and there is a good reason for it. There is the peace *with* God which comes through justification by faith alone. This is the knowledge that Jesus has paid your debt—peace with God—and you are assured that the wrath of God is not hovering over you, and you are saved. But there is the peace *of* God which comes from growth in grace. There comes a time when you discover that God is so real to you, that there is a peace that is *his* very peace. In fact in Colossians 3:15, some manuscripts read the *peace of Christ* instead of *peace of God* (see NIV). The point is that Jesus said, 'My peace I give to you'.

Now I want to bring out what I think is the crucial thing with regard to this matter of full assurance and I need to use a couple of terms to introduce this. The first is the word *objective* and then the word *subjective*. And I believe that by the time I have finished, you will see that it was necessary to use these terms.

By *objective* I mean what is *there*. By *subjective* it is what I *feel* or perceive is there. Let me give you an example of what I mean. There is a table at the front of an audience. If I were sitting in the back row, I would barely see that table. If you turned out the lights, nobody would see the table. It is still there, but you wouldn't perceive that it is there, you wouldn't feel it is there. Objectively the table is there all the time. Subjectively, when the lights are on, the audience can *see* that it is there, so they can also say, I feel it is there too. So what is there, and what they feel is there, are the same thing.

What does that have to do with full assurance? I'll tell you. What is objective is what the writer calls *hope*. He says in verse 11, 'We want each of you to show this same diligence... in order to make your hope *sure.*' 'Hope' has the definitive article in the Greek, but the subjective is, 'the *full assurance of* the hope'. The hope is there all the time, but whether I perceive it to be there is another matter. What is objective is the hope, what is subjective is my full assurance.

How do we know that the hope is there? Simply, when Jesus died on the cross, he paid the debt. When I believed on Jesus Christ, I transferred all hope that was in myself over to what he did for me on the cross. As a consequence, I had what the Puritans would call 'a saving interest' in that hope. But a full assurance is something that is even beyond that.

One may say, what could be more wonderful than knowing that you are saved and going to heaven? Let me answer this question. If one does not *eventually* come into what the Bible calls 'full assurance' (or whatever expression we could have used from the Bible), that person will almost certainly tend to lose what assurance he had, and will begin to doubt. So it is important that we come into this full assurance.

However, the person who comes into full assurance is not any 'more' saved than he or she was in the first place. This is why I said it is an objective hope, we can never lose that. But our perception of it is another matter. This is why the writer says, 'We want each of you ... to make your hope *sure*'.

Remedy for spiritual laziness

Now, why do it? Well he says in verse 12: 'We do not want you to become lazy.' In other words, it was the remedy for their dullness. Because they were dull of hearing, they had lost a sensitivity to spiritual things. This means that not to have this full assurance will make us slothful and dull. How we perceive what is there, the objective hope, will largely determine on whether we are slothful in our Christian living.

Full assurance is like when one can see clearly after the light has been turned on. There is nothing that will excite you and make the Bible more real to you and Jesus more real to you, than this full assurance, and it is the greatest motivation in the world.

What had happened to these Hebrew Christians? They had taken their eyes off Christ. We know that they had let external circumstances—persecution and looking back to the good old days—bring about a discouraged condition. What was the writer's advice to them? Well, back in 2:9 he said they must look to Jesus. In 4:14, he says, 'Therefore, since we have a great high priest who has gone through the heavens, Jesus, the Son of God'. And when he gets to chapter 12, it is looking to Jesus, keeping our eyes fixed on him. I have had many Christians who have come to see me with their problem of lack of assurance. In some cases, by telling them to look to Christ, it solved their problem.

Yet the writer knows that it is not as simple as just saying to a person, Look to Jesus. It is not simply trusting him for our salvation, but we must show the same *diligence* in seeking his face as these Christians had been showing at the practical level, trying to minister to people.

There is a verse in the Old Testament which says: 'If you will seek the Lord with all your heart, you will find him' (Jer. 29:13). But some of us, when it comes to our spiritual state and where we stand with the Lord, are not all that bothered about our intimate relationship with Christ. Occasionally we get exercised about it, but then things come that divert us and we lose interest. The writer knows that full assurance will come to those who so want to know the Lord that they seek for it with all diligence.

Imitators of spiritual heroes

However, full assurance is not only the remedy against being slothful, it is also what will put you into what I like to call 'the big leagues'. It comes to this: how much do you want to identify with the people that God has used?

Hebrews 11 describes the big league. Paul calls it being 'qualified to share in the inheritance of the saints in the kingdom of light' (Colossians 1:12). It is where you penetrate a sphere of action that is beyond what you would have, had you not given the same diligence to find that sure hope. You become a *follower of those* who have gone before you, who through faith and patience inherit the promises.

When I was a boy, my idol was a baseball player by the name of Joe DiMaggio. There was a time I actually combed my hair like he did. I went to see him play when he was the centre fielder of the New York Yankees. I watched every move that he made, and I started copying him. Yet I never made it into the big leagues; the most I ever did was play 'sand-lot' baseball. But there lies within my reach the possibility of being like one greater than a Joe DiMaggio!

Verse 12 highlights three things: who you can identify with, what they did, and how they did it.

Now if you want to know who they are, the writer lists some of them in chapter 11. In Cooperstown, New York, they have what they call the Hall of Fame, and Joe DiMaggio is in there with other great players. Well, Hebrews 11 is like that. We are given a description of what people did by faith. The wonderful thing is, though I could never be like Joe DiMaggio, much less look like him, or slide into the home plate like he did, I am told by the writer of Hebrews that I can be like Moses, I can be like Abraham, I can be like David. We discover how God looks at an individual, not how society looks at one. Any one of us can be like them, and I find this thrilling. We are able to identify with them. What did they do? They inherited the promises. And how did they do it? They inherited the promises through faith and patience.

'Followers' is a Greek word that means 'mimic' (the Greek word literally is *mimitae*). So the NIV translates it 'imitate'. There are two things that the Bible teaches and they are sort of opposites. One is that you ought to be yourself and you don't have to imitate people. But then there is also another strain in the Bible: pick a good model and follow that person. These seem to be contradictory principles, but let me try to explain.

It would be foolish for you to follow a person and try to imitate certain eccentricities that he might have. I also know what it is to imitate a preacher that I have admired and, you know, whenever a minister imitates a preacher, he will always pick up the bad points, and the odd things, and the eccentricities. Dr Lloyd-Jones once told me of a preacher in North Wales back in the twenties, who had an eccentric habit. His hair would get down on his face and he wouldn't take his hand and push it back, he would shake it back, and he did this all the time. And the Doctor said there were young preachers all over Wales who, as they preached, would copy this mannerism.

What the writer means when he says 'mimic' is that each of us is a follower of them as they are of Christ. That is what Paul said, 'Be followers of me as I am of Christ'. In other words, here is a promise. Come into this full assurance of hope and you will do in your generation what they did in theirs. It may not be recognised in our own generation, but neither were they in their generation.

We think that Isaiah must have been the Spurgeon of his day. You must have thought when you read the book of Isaiah, that a man who could say such beautiful things must surely have had thousands come to hear him? Isaiah was killed, they sawed his body in two. It is later generations who talk about Isaiah. So to be a follower of Isaiah doesn't mean you are to try and produce the rhetoric and the literature and the prose of Isaiah. This full assurance will bring you to the place where you are in tune with Isaiah's God who will say, 'I have a plan for you. You are not going to be able to speak like Isaiah; you are not going to have his ability; you won't be a Spurgeon or a Martyn Lloyd-Jones, but I am going to do something with you.'

Here's the joy. You will be like these great men in that none of them could do exactly like those before them. Hebrews 11 describes men of faith, every single one of whom had to do something different from the one who went before. They weren't able to do like it was done in the previous generation. This is the way we are going to imitate them—we are faithful in our generation as they were in theirs.

Inheriting the promises

There is something very thrilling here. What is an heir? He is one that inherits, in that he takes possession of what was owned by a person who died, by virtue of that person's last will and testament. What is it then that every Christian inherits, through faith and patience, by virtue of Christ's death?

What is guaranteed by faith plus nothing? Salvation.

What is guaranteed through faith plus patience? Things that *accompany* salvation. Hebrews 6:9: 'Dear friends, we are confident of better things in your case—things that accompany salvation.' In other words, *inheriting the promises*.

What then is inheriting the promises? 2 Peter 1:4 says that God 'has given us his very great and precious promises, so that through them you may participate in the divine nature and escape the corruption in the world caused by evil desires.' We are not talking about one promise, but many.

What are the promises? I am going to list twelve; I initially had four or five beginning with the letter 'S', so I decided to make them all 'S's'.

(1) It means the promise of *Strength*. Said Moses, 'As thy days, so shall thy strength be'. 'I can do all things through Christ who strengthens me.'

(2) There is the promise that God will *Supply* all we need. If you have a financial problem, you need to know that you are going to inherit this promise, that it is yours, that you take possession of it, that God will supply your need.

(3) The promise of *Safety*. This is what the Psalmist said. Let me remind you of a verse from Psalm 91: 'Surely he will save you from the fowler's snare, and from the deadly pestilence' (v. 3).

(4) There is the promise of *Sealing*, where we have the sealing of the Holy Spirit.

(5) Then there is *Security*, the promise that God is going to take care of us and give us security.

(6) It means the promise of *Service*. Are you afraid that you are not going to be used by the Lord? Are you afraid that your gift won't be discovered? Are you afraid that somehow you are not going to be of any use? You can inherit the promise of Service. God wants you, but you will not be used, or be worth anything, unless you are giving all diligence, giving the same diligence to make your hope sure.

(7) There is the promise of *Stability*. You see, the double-minded man is unstable in all his ways (Jas. 1:8).

(8) The promise of being *Settled*. 1 Peter 5:10, 'After you have suffered a little while, [God] will himself restore you and make you strong, firm and *steadfast*.' God will settle you.

(9) There is the promise that God will be your *Shield*. We sing about this in Psalm 84: 'the Lord God is a sun and shield'.

(10) He also promises to be your *Shelter* (Psalm 27:5).

(11) The promise of *Sympathy*: Jesus is touched with the feeling of our weaknesses (Heb. 4:15).

(12) The promise of *Surprises*. 'No eye has seen, no ear has heard, no mind has conceived what God has prepared for those who love him' (1 Cor. 2:9).

So that inheriting the promises is to do in our day what great believers have done in theirs. It is appropriating the promises in such a way that we possess them and we say, they are mine.

How is it done?

The answer is: through faith and patience. Do you see the distinction? Salvation is by faith plus *nothing*; inheriting the promises is by faith plus *patience*.

In Hebrews 11:6 the writer says, 'Anyone who comes to him [God] must believe that he exists' (what would you call that— faith? I would). But he goes on to say, 'and that he rewards those who earnestly seek him' (I would call that 'patience').

What will happen? Well, what has always been there *objectively*. We discover how real God is, how true the Bible is, the simplicity of it, and the death of Jesus on the cross will become more real to us than ever. The interesting thing is that the more we grow and the more we learn, the simpler it becomes. We realise that Jesus paid our debt and we know this and full assurance is there, and we begin to inherit the promises and see how God is with us in every walk of our lives.

19

The Promise
And God's Oath

When God made his promise to Abraham, since there was no-one greater for him to swear by, he swore by himself, saying, 'I will surely bless you and give you many descendants.' And so after waiting patiently, Abraham received what was promised (Hebrews 6:13-15).

When the writer says, 'For when God made his promise to Abraham', what is this all about? He has just said that we should be followers of those 'who through faith and patience inherit what has been promised.' But it is obvious that though he says 'imitators of those', and though in Hebrews 11 he is going to mention a number of people, Abraham is on his mind. He is the main example, and in Hebrews 11 Abraham gets more attention than anyone else.

We approach this section by going from the general to the particular. Looking at it generally, here are verses that refer, first of all, to the *faithfulness of God*. He is faithful who promised. One of the things the Devil will try to undermine, if he can, is your belief that God will keep his word. So here is a section that brings us face to face with the absolute faithfulness of God. He will not let you down.

Secondly, *the absolute supremacy of God*. There is none greater. 'Since there was no-one greater for him to swear by, he swore by himself.' What was left? Is God going to swear by his own creation? Has he got to pull somebody out of nowhere and swear by them? There is no one, because all that there is, is himself, plus what he has made, and so he swears by himself. And we need to understand this. The Devil would undermine the absolute supremacy of God. But the Devil himself is under God. The Devil is beneath God. The Devil cannot defeat God.

Remember this. God is going to have his way—a wonderful thing to realise.

And the third thing that this section teaches us is the *integrity of God*. Later on the writer is going to say, it is impossible for God to lie. I once preached a sermon using three 'L's' for three things God cannot do: he cannot learn, because he already knows everything; he cannot lose, because he is God; and he cannot lie.

Let's move to the particular: it is the story of Abraham and Isaac, one of the most famous stories of the Bible. We are going to learn something of the nature of God's oath. It is important to see that there is a difference between his promise and his oath.

We also need to see the reward for obedience. Now this is something that I think is neglected. The Bible teaches that there is a reward for obedience—God stoops to our level, to motivate us. So what is the reward? Well, we see in the case of Abraham, that he had been promised something, and in verse 15 we read, 'After he had waited patiently, he received the promise'.

The writer is encouraging us to believe that there is something available for all Christians, but which these Hebrews have seemed to come short of. Now, if you have been a Christian for any length of time at all, it is a happy discovery to know that God wants to bless us more than ever. There is a deeper level of knowing God, when God becomes more real, and his word becomes more revealing, and there comes a time when we are excited about the Lord in a way we hadn't been before. I believe A W Tozer was right when he said, 'You can have as much of God as you want.'

All right. What is 'inheriting what has been promised?' I'm going to put it like this. It is seeing God work. It is experiencing the reality of God's power while we are alive. There are some who think the only way you are going to know that is after you die. Not so, says the writer, there is such a thing as inheriting the promises in this life!

When God guaranteed the promise to Abraham

Immediately after the crowning trial of Abraham's life, that is, when he would have sacrificed Isaac, we see that God in heaven could not contain his joy, as it were, over what Abraham had done. For when God saw that Abraham was willing to sacrifice his only son, Isaac, we are told that the Lord came back a second time, and said, 'I swear' (Gen. 22:16). And there it is, the oath. Up to now, it had been promise, promise, promise, promise, promise, but this was the crowning triumph: the oath. The worst thing Abraham had to endure was over, and God was so moved that he made an oath.

What did this guarantee? It guaranteed that Abraham would inherit the promises. How was it guaranteed? Well, by God's oath.

In Genesis 12:2-3, there is the first promise to Abraham: 'I will make you into a great nation and I will bless you; I will make your name great, and you will be a blessing. I will bless those who bless you, and whoever curses you I will curse; and all peoples on earth will be blessed through you.'

In Genesis 13:15-16, there is the second promise given to Abraham: 'All the land that you see I will give to you and your offspring for ever. I will make your offspring like the dust of the earth, so that if anyone could count the dust, then your offspring could be counted.'

In Genesis 15:5-6, there is the third promise to Abraham: 'He took him outside and said, "Look up at the heavens and count the stars—if indeed you can count them." Then he said to him, "So shall your offspring be." Abram believed the LORD, and he credited it to him as righteousness.'

In verse 18 of Genesis 15: 'On that day the LORD made a covenant with Abram and said, "To your descendants I give this land, from the river of Egypt to the great river, the Euphrates"...'. That's another promise.

In chapter 17:7-8, there is a further promise: 'I will establish my covenant as an everlasting covenant between me and you and your descendants after you for the generations to come, to be your God and the God of your descendants after you. The whole land of Canaan, where you are now an alien, I will give as an everlasting possession to you and your descendants after you; and I will be their God.'

Again in verses 15-16: 'As for Sarai your wife, you are no longer to call her Sarai; her name will be Sarah. I will bless her and will surely give you a son by her. I will bless her so that she will be the mother of nations; kings of peoples will come from her.'

Lastly, in verse 21: 'But my covenant I will establish with Isaac, whom Sarah will bear to you by this time next year.'

Here are a series of promises. Why are they listed like that? Because God knew that Abraham needed reassurance along the way and so he kept giving him another promise. But these promises are much the same as those he had received already. Remember that Abraham is walking by faith all this time, he has not seen anything happen yet. But he is believing it.

Many believers are like that. God has given them a word and they believe him. And then they get discouraged, and say, 'Lord, really, really, help me!' And he comes back, and what is it? Same old word. And they think, 'When are you going to do something, Lord?' And he just gives the same word. But it strengthens them and they say, 'Well, praise the Lord. I'll just trust his word. I'm going on, I'm going to believe you.'

Now there comes a time when they need to see something happen and God knows that. Sometimes when they think they need to have that breakthrough, he just gives them another promise. But there is a time when Christians need to see more.

In Genesis 18:18-19, we read: 'Abraham will surely become a great and powerful nation, and all nations on earth will be blessed through him. For I have chosen him, so that he will direct his children and his household after him to keep the way of the LORD by doing what is right and just, so that the LORD will bring about for Abraham what he has promised him.'

Finally, in chapter 21:12: 'God said to him [Abraham], "Do not be so distressed about the boy and your maidservant. Listen to whatever Sarah tells you, because it is through Isaac that your offspring will be reckoned."' Not Ishmael, but Isaac.

Each of these promises were trials that needed a kind of seal. What God did was to give Abraham *another* promise upon the top of the *promise* he had already. So what we have up to now is promise after promise, until finally Abraham actually saw God at work, when Isaac came along. Then it was obvious that God had stepped in. The apostle Paul picks up on this when referring to Abraham in Romans 4:18-21:

> Against all hope, Abraham in hope believed and so became the father of many nations, just as it had been said to him, 'So shall your offspring be.' Without weakening in his faith, he faced the fact that his body was as good as dead—since he was about a hundred years old—and that Sarah's womb was also dead. Yet he did not waver through unbelief regarding the promise of God, but was strengthened in his faith and gave glory to God, being fully persuaded that God had power to do what he had promised.

Abraham had behaved, if I may put it like that, marvellously up to then. I am not saying that there were not blemishes in Abraham's life—he made some mistakes, he was not perfect. We know what happened when he went into Egypt with Sarah, how later he slept with Hagar. But other than these, generally speaking, Abraham just moved on, trusting God.

Now why does the writer bring in Abraham? Many of these Hebrew Christians had been saved for thirty years. Yet when he talks about God's rest, they say, 'Well, I don't know anything about that. I've prayed for this and nothing's ever happened to me.' So he brings in Abraham. We all know about Abraham's faith, but do we want to persevere and endure, and keep believing? We want God to do something and when he gives us another word, do we just believe it? That pleases God and yet the oath hasn't come yet.

Why is the oath so important? There's a difference between the promise and the oath. The promise, in itself, is sufficient, in that it is God's word and it is impossible for God to lie. But the writer is going to talk about *two* immutable things in which it is impossible for God to lie—the promise *and* the oath. Now, the promise is conditional; the oath is unconditional and irrevocable. As long as God is promising you don't need to worry. You just do as he says and he's going to keep his word. But when he swears, nothing can stop it. That seals it, it makes it irrevocable. God takes over, it is as though Abraham is out of the picture altogether. That's how absolute it is.

The point that the writer wants to make is that up to now God's word had come via promises, but now there is something new: it is his oath.

Up to Genesis 22, Abraham had endured as much as you would expect anybody ever to go through; he has trusted God in circumstances that would throw most people. But the worst ordeal ever known up to then by any man on the face of the earth (and I don't know of anything that is its equivalent since our Lord's dying on the cross), is described in Genesis 22. We read that God said to Abraham, 'Take your son, your only son Isaac, whom you love, and go to the region of Moriah. Sacrifice him there as a burnt offering.'

When you realise that Isaac is the only link between Abraham and this nation that is going to be as populous as dust, that God has clearly said, 'It is through Isaac that your offspring will be reckoned', then God's demand that Abraham take Isaac and kill him didn't add up.

Here may be the key for many of you who have come so far in spiritual blessing, and then come up to a place which you never get past. Why? Simply because God gives you a command that makes no sense to you. Even though you know he is saying it, you say, Surely not! I just don't see it. And you back off and you never come into the blessing that God has in mind.

You rationalise it. You might say, 'Can you see Abraham going for pastoral counselling?' His counsellor would say, 'God wouldn't tell you to do that!' Yet whenever God has something extraordinary for us to do, it will always be that which, humanly speaking, we could deny as really being of God. Most of us don't need a lot of convincing anyway. Anything that can persuade us to back off, we're ready for it. But Abraham went on.

So I wonder if this is the key for some who have never come into the full assurance, simply because you have gone so far and then come up to something you just rationalised away—'No way could *that* be God's word to me.'

Here are some principles for you.

The first is this: God often requires what makes no sense—'Take your son, your only son Isaac'.

Secondly, we are asked to obey the Holy Spirit one day at a time without getting the final details. Because God says, 'Sacrifice him there as a burnt offering on one of the mountains *I will tell you about*', Abraham might say, 'Well, wait a minute, tell me where I am going.' 'No,' God says, 'you just start; as you get closer, then I'll tell you.' Many of us say, 'I want to know the bottom line, right now. Tell me how it's going to turn out. Where will I be? Will I marry this person? Will I be in this position? Will I get to do this?' 'Look,' God says, 'you start and I'll tell you when you get there.' God doesn't lead us directly from A to Z; he leads us from A to B; B to C. And this is what Abraham is doing; no murmuring, no complaining.

Thirdly, the darkest hour is just before dawn. I cannot imagine a more painful ordeal in the world, than for Isaac, this little boy—we don't know exactly how old he was, but he was old enough to know what was happening. He said, 'Father, I see the wood, I see the fire, where's the lamb?' What must it have done to Abraham to have to say, 'God will provide'?

The writer of Hebrews tells us that Abraham was convinced that God was simply going to raise Isaac from the dead (Heb. 11:19). Abraham thought he was going to kill Isaac and God was going to bring him back to life. So he went through with it, and he had the knife in his hand with his son tied on the altar when the angel told him not to proceed. God says, Now I know that you love me.

And that is when we have the hope, for we read in Genesis

22:15-17, 'The angel of the LORD called unto Abraham from heaven a second time and said, "I swear by myself, declares the LORD, that because you have done this and have not withheld your son, your only son, I will surely bless you and make your descendants as numerous as the stars in the sky and as the sand on the seashore."'

Let me say this: if you seek the Lord with all your heart, you'll find him. Do you want God to be real to you? It means you're going to have to obey him. It will be costly. No faith is brought to maturity without suffering. Just think, God has called you into a sphere where you can be the spiritual equivalent of Abraham. Any one of us can do it by just being faithful.

20

What Does
It Mean For
God To Swear?

When God made his promise to Abraham, since there was no-one greater for him to swear by, he swore by himself, saying, 'I will surely bless you and give you many descendants.' And so after waiting patiently, Abraham received what was promised (Hebrews 6:13-15).

The answer is: to affirm by an oath, to ensure credibility. In a law court a witness will affirm his testimony by an oath by putting one hand on the Bible and raising the other heavenward.

In the Old Testament different individuals made oaths. For example, in 1 Kings 2:23, we read, 'Then King Solomon swore by the LORD: "May God deal with me, be it ever so severely, if Adonijah does not pay with his life for this request!"' Jezebel did something similar in 1 Kings 19:2, 'Jezebel sent a messenger to Elijah to say, "May the gods deal with me, be it ever so severely, if by this time tomorrow I do not make your life like that of one of them."' She swore that she was going to kill Elijah. It was the common way in the Old Testament, an appeal in order to support the intensity of one's earnestness. An oath, to be an oath, must rest on a higher authority.

The many promises God made to Abraham were confirmed by an oath. But whose oath? Would you believe it was God's oath?

A number of questions arise which I want to explore.

Why mention Abraham?
Why does the writer bring in Abraham? Here is something fundamental to a brand-new Christian, to a young Christian, to an old Christian—why mention Abraham? Because the gospel

was preached in advance to Abraham (Gal. 3:8).

In Romans 4, Abraham was Paul's example for the doctrine of justification by faith alone. In John 8:56, Jesus referred to Abraham and said, 'Your father Abraham rejoiced at the thought of seeing my day; he saw it and was glad.' Why? Because all that Jesus came to do was revealed to Abraham. This is an extraordinary thing to realise.

I can think of nothing pertinent by way of how a person becomes a Christian, or in the living of the Christian life, that is not found somewhere in the life of Abraham. It is a thought, isn't it? I may be wrong, but I believe you will find that to be the case. I won't make a big point of it, but I am saying this, if you are a new Christian and you are looking for an Old Testament model, here's your man—Abraham.

Why would God need to swear at all?

This one is more difficult to answer. God is truth and his word should be enough. Why would God swear if he is already true in himself, and it is impossible for God to lie?

I therefore checked every commentary. One of them is by William Gouge, a great Puritan. He gave three reasons why God would swear at all.

The first reason is that God *condescended to the weakness of man*, for God knew that his bare promise may still leave us doubting. God knew that man needed more support. As the Psalmist put it: 'He knows how we are formed; he remembers that we are dust' (Ps. 103:14).

The second reason William Gouge gave was: God's oath was *needful and useful for Isaac*, who was involved at that moment. Isaac, when Abraham was offering him as a sacrifice, needed this. He would need it in his own day, because there would come a time when Abraham would be gone, and the seed would be continuing through Isaac. Isaac needed to be able to lean back on the fact of God's oath.

The third reason, according to William Gouge, is that God's oath was *needful and useful for the seed of Abraham*, from generation to generation, namely the church. As Paul wrote, 'those who believe are children of Abraham'. We depend on the oath of God to Abraham.

I have a fourth reason that I don't think anybody would question. My answer would be: *to teach us more of the ways of God.* For God is never untrue to himself. He reveals himself on purpose. And what he reveals about himself is never by accident. God never makes an unguarded comment.

To whom will God swear?

The only answer is, he had to swear by himself, because there is no higher authority.

Donald Guthrie, in his commentary, makes an astute comment. He says, 'When the writer said because he could swear by no greater, it was tantamount to saying that his own word was good enough.' But we are going to go into it deeper yet. If God's word was good enough, why should the oath be believed any more than the promise? Is it not true that if you can't believe a man's word, neither are you going to believe him when he swears? What's the answer to this? I have three suggestions.

First, it is through the oath that God *lets us see his heart*, and the intensity of his feelings which otherwise might not be known. In the case of Abraham, he swore in mercy, and as Philip Edgecumbe Hughes says in his commentary, 'God swore in mercy in response to Abraham's obedience.' This is an important point to keep in mind, realising that an oath is something God does in response to a situation on earth. The promise comes of his own free will, and he does it without respect to what man might do. But the oath comes in response to something that has happened and God, in responding to what is going on below, will sometimes swear.

In the case of Abraham, he swore in mercy: 'I will surely bless you and make your descendants as numerous as the stars in the sky and as the sand on the seashore.'

But take the case of the Children of Israel, who, having kept the Passover and crossed the Red Sea on dry land, came into the wilderness. The time came when they were only eleven days journey from Canaan, so they sent some spies to look over the land. The spies came back, and said, 'It is no use, we can never do it.' But one of them, Caleb, said, 'Why, we can! We can do it because it is God who is going to do it; it is God that has brought us this far.' Caleb was outnumbered, he lost. But in heaven God responded to what went on below. He didn't swear in his mercy, he swore in his wrath, and said, 'They shall not enter into my rest,' and they didn't. They died in the wilderness. Their carcasses, said the writer to the Hebrews, were found in the wilderness.

Why then would God swear at all? The first answer that I am giving here is: through the oath, God lets us see his heart and the intensity of his feelings.

There is a second reason I put before you: God makes an oath *to show he has now taken things into hand by himself*. On one side the *promise*, on the other side, *oath*. I want us to see the difference. The first is that the promise is general, the oath is particular. Now I mean by that, the promise is general without respect to what men or women might do. It is a free offer, generally, as the gospel is. But the oath is particular, and refers to when a person *has* responded below and the situation therefore merits a response from above, and the oath that God swears in heaven is in response to what went on below. So if a person refuses to believe the gospel, God in heaven swears in his wrath. If the person believes, he swears in his mercy.

In addition, the promise is conditional; for example: 'God so loved the world that he gave his one and only Son, that whoever believes in him shall not perish but have eternal life.' The promise is *if* you believe. But when it comes to the oath, what we have is that it is unconditional, it is irrevocable. Why? Because once God has sworn, it is all over.

God swore concerning those who disagreed with Caleb, 'I declared on oath in my anger, they shall never enter my rest.' There was nothing they could do about it. The very next day they came to Moses, and said, 'We see now that we should have gone on. We are sorry.' God said, 'It's too late; you had your chance yesterday.' He had already sworn. Awful! So an oath is irrevocable; a promise is conditional.

I have not found any commentary that goes into this as deeply as I think we could go into it. It is a marvellous thing here to see, when God swears, it is all over. Up until then, we are praying, 'Lord, are you going to step in or not? What's going to happen? Lord, help us!' But then, God steps in and he swears. He might swear in mercy and if he does, nothing's going to stop it. If he says, I swore in my anger, it is impossible for them to be renewed again unto repentance.

There is a third reason why God swore: to show that he *is going to act at once.* There will be no further delay. When a promise is given, its fulfilment can linger. God made a promise to Abraham in Genesis 12 that was renewed over ten times, a little different each time. When we get to Genesis 22, it's an oath, not a promise. What does that mean? It means no delay. And so, God at once provided the lamb for Abraham. This is the beauty of it: with the promise we wait, generations wait; but the proof that God was acting at once (he swore)—there was the lamb caught in the thicket. And so, when he swears in his wrath, the Children of Israel died in the wilderness.

Let me show you something else that's thrilling. In Luke 1, Zechariah, the father of John the Baptist, filled with the Holy Spirit, prophesied and referred to 'the oath he [God] swore to our father Abraham: to rescue us from the hand of our enemies, and to enable us to serve him without fear in holiness and righteousness before him all our days. And you, my child, will be called the prophet of the Most High' (vv. 73-76). Here was the oath disclosed. What did it mean?

It meant something was going to happen. No more delays. Over five hundred years had passed since Isaiah prophesied, 'A virgin will be with child and will give birth to a son'; about four hundred years since Malachi, the last Old Testament prophet before Christ. For four hundred years there was barrenness, with just a remnant. Was God ever going to speak? Then came

Zechariah, filled with the Holy Spirit and he referred to the oath: no more delay. John the Baptist, the forerunner, was on the way, he was soon to be born, and Jesus, the Messiah, was coming. Within the year they would have the Messiah. The time had come.

Why is this relevant for our lives?

Are we dealing here with something that is just theoretical? Are we talking about something that is detached from us, or does this study on the difference between the promise of God and God's oath, have any relevance?

If there is a Christian who wants to know something about *assurance of salvation*, this is related. I was talking on one occasion to someone who couldn't believe that we could know that we would finally be saved. This person, a sincere Christian I am sure, was convinced that we can know we are saved now, but we could not know that we will be saved ten years from now or that we are going to be in heaven. As I have repeated several times already, the promise assures you that you will go to heaven. But then is there such a thing as knowing absolutely that you are going to go to heaven?

Is there such a thing as *knowing God will answer your prayer*? John says there is, 'If we know that he hears us—whatever we ask—we know that we have what we asked of him' (1 John 5:15). So if you want to know if God is going to answer your prayer, well you would certainly be interested in this study.

And thirdly, *the question of guidance*. How is it going to turn out? Will all be well?

I would have thought that those three things relate to every Christian, that there is encouragement to anybody who has been seeking the Lord. You may be undergoing right now a great trial, the greatest trial you have ever known. Abraham having to sacrifice his only son was the greatest trial he had ever known, but by trusting the Lord right through it and being obedient unto the end, he was given, as a consequence, something that was greater than he had ever experienced in his life. You can be sure that if you are in a trial at the moment when you don't understand the way God is leading you, in fact what he has asked of you makes no sense and goes against what you thought he was promising you previously, God says, 'Trust me.' It may be that you will experience what Abraham experienced, seeing God swear in his mercy.

What did the oath do? Well, in verse 17 we have the answer: it confirmed the promise. 'Because God wanted to make the unchanging nature of his purpose very clear to the heirs of what was promised, he confirmed it with an oath.' God's oath was something he carried out in advance of Abraham's seed being as the sand of the seashore. It would take generations before that promise could be confirmed outwardly, physically, externally. Why should Abraham have believed it any more than when he believed promise after promise after promise?

Here's the answer: it is as though the future becomes the present. This, in a sense, is the essence of what makes an oath, an oath. God can swear and we believe it, infallibly and perfectly and absolutely. How is that possible? Because when one is enabled to see God swear, it is as though we are brought right up into the heavens, where there is no past, present or future, and the future becomes present; it is as though we are already in the future because we are in the presence of God. When you are in the presence of God, the future is present, and you believe it. That's what happened. This is the difference between God's promise and his oath, it is as though the future becomes present.

What does this mean? Concerning assurance of salvation, you have been carried up into heaven. You know you are going to be in heaven some day; it is as though you have already been there. That's how sure you are.

You can have the same thing happen in prayer. Where you know you have prayed in the will of God, you know in advance how something is going to turn out.

It is so with guidance. Will you come out on the other side? Are you in trial at the moment, and you can't see clearly? When

Paul was in the Mediterranean Sea during the storm (Acts 27), God came to him and said, 'Cheer up, Paul, you're going to make it.' And Paul went to the crew and said, 'I believe God and it will be just as he told me.' The oath is where you just know in advance how it is going to turn out.

When it comes to these things, some people are quite content just to know that they have an interest in Christ. They want to tick off the various signs that prove they have been saved. But Hebrews 6 is geared for those who want to see something close up and want to go and investigate. Jesus said, 'I am the gate; whoever enters through me will be saved. He will come in and go out, and *find pasture*... I have come that they may have life, and have it *to the full*' (John 10:9-10).

A detailed summary

I want to summarise the differences between the promise and the oath to try and help us understand when it comes to assurance, answered prayer and guidance. I have come up with ten distinctions.

(1) The promise is like *a priori,* a prior assumption with which you proceed. An oath however, is *a posteriori* which is clearly revealed. So that the oath is what has been given to you as a present reality, and from then on it is something you look back upon.

(2) A promise is general, universal and impersonal. But the oath is particular, limited and personal.

(3) A promise is conditional, whereas the oath is irrevocable.

(4) The promise is open: I would put the little word 'if' as almost always involved with promise. But the oath is closed: once the oath has been uttered by God it is a closed issue. If he swears in his mercy, it is irrevocable, nothing can ever change it, you are eternally saved. If he swears in his wrath, 'they shall not enter my rest', nothing can be done to change that.

(5) The promise has to do with waiting. Most of the promises say, Wait on the Lord, whereas the oath is experiencing.

(6) The promise is to be trusted, and could be renewed, but the

oath has been confirmed by God.

(7) The promise points to the future, whereas the oath is the future made present.

(8) The promise refers to what I would call general knowledge. But the oath is sure knowledge.

(9) The promise is enduring with patience and the oath is obtaining the promise. That's the writer's language in verse 15: 'After Abraham patiently endured, he obtained the promise.' He is using that expression to mean the oath. It was the oath that had been promised all along, as Abraham was to see in the end.

(10) The promise is seeing far off and it also can mean that its fulfilment may be far off. The oath, however, means something is at hand. If God gives you the breakthrough with regard to prayer or guidance, or some matter, it is very likely that something is going to happen soon.

It happened in Lewis

Recently I listened to a tape recording of Duncan Campbell talking about the Hebridean Revival.

One of the things he mentioned was that two elderly ladies who had a burden for the Isle of Lewis prayed, waiting on God for months for they vowed they would give no rest nor peace to the Almighty until he granted their request for revival! One night, these two ladies together had a vision, when they saw the parish church with people, including young folk, streaming into it.

Four miles away at precisely the same time, seven men were praying in a barn. They were just praying together when one of them read out loud, 'Who shall ascend to the hill of the LORD? He that hath clean hands and a pure heart.' And the Spirit of God came upon them and they were prostrate on their faces. Three of the men went into a trance.

They told the parish minister; the result was that they invited Duncan Campbell to come over for a mission, and they wanted him in two weeks time. But Duncan Campbell wrote back, 'I will put this in my diary for next year, I can't come just now.'

They wrote back and said, 'You will be here, for God has told us you will be here.'

At the same time another letter came cancelling a mission he was due to attend the same week. So he went to Lewis, roughly two weeks after the vision, and after the seven men prayed. They had a service and nothing happened at all. At nine o'clock, as the last person was leaving, one of the brethren came up to Duncan Campbell, and said, 'Well, I hope you're not discouraged nothing's happened tonight.'

They were just walking out the door when suddenly the same man started praying, and he started saying this: 'Lord, your honour is at stake; Lord, your honour is at stake.' And he repeated this for about five minutes and suddenly he was struck prostrate on the floor in a trance. When Duncan Campbell walked outside he estimates there were five to six hundred people standing there. There had been maybe three hundred in the service and the service was over. But there were five to six hundred outside, he doesn't know how they knew to be there. They decided to come back in and the service lasted till four o'clock in the morning.

It went on like that for five weeks. One time they were going down the street and found two or three hundred people outside the police station, praying, and the Spirit of God was coming on prisoners, and as they walked through, there were people on the highway, bowing, and kneeling in prayer.

The oath was given to the two ladies. When God swears and lets you see it, it means something is about to happen.

The difference between a promise and an oath is this: let's say you need a pardon and you go to the Queen. She receives you and she says to you, 'I will grant the pardon.' Then she says to you, 'But I won't announce it until next Wednesday.' Do you wait until next Wednesday to be happy about it? Or do you know now you are going to have it? That's the thing. When the oath comes, you believe that you have it and shall receive it.

Or to put it another way. Do you know the day I passed my driving test was one of the happiest days of my life? When the instructor said at the end, 'Congratulations, Mr Kendall, you've passed,' I rejoiced all day long. But I didn't get the driving licence itself in the post for another two months.

What we are talking about is that the knowledge is so real to you that you go ahead and rejoice in it. I know I am going to go to heaven when I die, but when I get there I will love that too.

21

**Letting
God
Be God**

When God made his promise to Abraham, since there was no-one greater for him to swear by, he swore by himself, saying, 'I will surely bless you and give you many descendants.' And so after waiting patiently, Abraham received what was promised. Men swear by someone greater than themselves, and the oath confirms what is said and puts an end to all argument. Because God wanted to make the unchanging nature of his purpose very clear to the heirs of what was promised, he confirmed it with an oath (Hebrews 6:13-17).

In this chapter we look first at the content of the oath God swore to Abraham: 'I will surely bless you and make your descendants as numerous as the stars in the sky and as the sand on the seashore.' There's more to it than that as we will see a little later from Genesis 22, but for now, we will concentrate on these words.

The first thing to notice is that the content of the oath did not differ from the content of the promise. So, if you are asking what is the difference between the promise and the oath, I tell you this, it is not in the content. For what God swore was but what he had already promised, and this is another reason why we say full assurance doesn't make a person more saved than he always was. The oath gave to Abraham the highest form of assurance. It is like the sealing of the Spirit on faith. It was still the same word of God. But Abraham, you could say, believed more than ever, because he saw things more clearly than ever.

Blessing

In the content of the oath, the first aspect to notice is the blessing: 'I will surely bless you.' Now, as I said, there is nothing new here because in Genesis 12, where God spoke to Abraham for the first time, he said, 'I will make you into a great nation and I will bless you; I will make your name great and you will be a blessing.' It is repeated in Genesis 17:16. The word, *bless*, has been a part of the promise all along.

Now when he says, 'I will surely bless you' or 'Blessing I will bless thee' (AV), he is using a Hebrew expression. Yet, I think there is much more to it than that, and that is what we are going to spend some time with. It is a present participle so although something was happening at the time to Abraham, he was having it both ways. Something was going on right then between God and Abraham, but that was not all, something was yet to happen as well. It was a promise of the future too.

It was not only hearing the word, but we could say it was an internal spontaneous combustion. Something happened, and it put an end to all strife. For all of those years Abraham had been getting promise after promise after promise. But there came a day when it was an oath. It was the same content; it was the same word, it was blessing, but there was something about it that ended everything for ever and ever, and from now on, Abraham knew that God had stepped in. God says, 'Abraham, move over, I am taking over.' And Abraham could just cease from his works.

This is what is meant in Hebrews 4:10: 'Anyone who enters God's rest also rests from his own work'. It is where the striving is over and you just rest in God. That's what God wants us to do, and yet we tend not to do it even when we get an encouraging word from God.

What did Abraham feel? The answer is that everything was now completely taken out of his hands. Before Isaac came, Abraham thought, 'Well, what am I going to do?' for he was getting older. When he was seventy years of age, God said, 'You're going to have offspring as the sand of the sea.' Yet nothing was happening. Poor old Abraham thought, 'Sarah's not going to have a child. I can see that, she's too old. God told me he was going to do it.' When Sarah said, 'Here's my handmaid, Hagar, lie with her,' Abraham said, 'All right, I'll do that.' Sure enough Hagar had a son, and Abraham said, 'God's word has been kept, and he's going to have his promise fulfilled through me after all.' My point is, Abraham was able to do all of that, *making* it work out; he was still trying to control events.

Abraham needed to learn that God will keep his word absolutely. Even after Isaac had come, Abraham needed that lesson, and it wasn't until Abraham began to take God so seriously that he would sacrifice his own son because he believed God that much, that God said, 'Now I see that you really believe my word.' God will swear in his mercy, when we come to the place where we really believe indeed.

So when God swore, Abraham felt that God had taken over. The blessing was, *I* will do it, *I* will do it. All those years Abraham thought he had to do something. It is the most wonderful thing in the world to realise that God by himself has promised to supply your need.

On the other hand, what if what we want doesn't happen? It may be that we are asking for something that God says, 'I can't let you have.' Will we still love God as much? Maybe we are praying for this person to be healed, or we are wanting that event to take place.

I heard something once that really gripped my heart, and I want to share it with you. There is a minister in America whose name is Adrian Rogers, pastor of the Bellevue Baptist Church, Memphis, Tennessee. He is a great man, one of the giants holding forth biblical inerrancy in the Southern Baptist Convention. He told about a couple who had a baby. Before the baby became much of a child it took ill, so they prayed for their baby's healing. Oh, did they pray! Yet they had to become reconciled to the fact that their baby was going to die. And the baby died. You can go to the graveyard today and find the tombstone. It has the baby's name, date of birth, date of death, and then two words: 'Yes, Lord'. They became reconciled. Even if we want to see God do something, we must be reconciled to what his will is.

But in the case of Abraham, he had a clear case, because God said, 'I will bless you.' Remember God is not going to swear according to mercy, if it goes against his word. Don't expect to get any kind of breakthrough from God when it goes right against his word. But this was a case where the word was there for he had already said, I will bless you. So, here it is, God says, 'I will take over, it's my job, you get out of the picture.'

When a person is in the Spirit, he or she is often able to perceive what God is doing in heaven. When Peter and John came up to the Gate Beautiful, where the forty-year-old lame man was, having never walked a day in his life, they said, 'In the name of Jesus Christ of Nazareth, rise up and walk!' (Acts 3). They knew that was what was going to happen. There was no question in their minds. But the trouble with so many of us today, and so much that goes on under the name of healing, is that when the praying is made, there is no assurance that it is going to happen at all. Sometimes they try to work it up psychologically, and say, 'Well, claim it, and just believe.' But there was none of that with Peter and John.

They knew that God was going to do something right then, and they could just walk up to the man and say, 'Give me your hand. Stand up!' What fools they would have been if the guy stood up and fell back down! Today they would blame it on the man and say, 'You don't have faith!' He didn't have any faith at all, but Peter and John knew that God was going to do something right then. Why? Simultaneously they were given witness that God was going to do it—that's swearing in mercy.

An example of swearing in wrath is when Peter said to Ananias, 'Why have you lied to the Holy Spirit?' And he dropped dead (Acts 5). Three hours later and Peter said to Sapphira, 'The same men who buried your husband are going to carry you out.' What if she had lived? Could Peter have said, 'Well I guess I got one wrong!' No. Peter knew that God had sworn in his wrath and he acted right then.

Sometimes God will give that kind of perception to a person. If we do ever have real revival, I think that we will see some of that.

But there was more. Abraham not only had the internal feeling, but there was the external carrying out of the promise. From now on, Abraham could sit back, as it were, and watch it all happen before his eyes. What a load off Abraham's shoulders, when he saw that God was going to do it. It was as if God had said to Abraham, 'Will you quit worrying about your descendants? I'm the one who told you about this. If I'm the one who told you that I am going to carry it out, it's my problem.'

Every minister needs to realise this about his church, that the church is God's church. Westminster Chapel isn't my church, it's not the deacons' church, it's God's church. And he will add to the church; it is his work. But what a great feeling when God just says to me, 'R. T., you're worrying too much about this, you're just trying too hard. Would you just step aside and see what happens when I do it?' That's the principle.

So God said to Abraham, 'I will multiply you' ('make your descendants numerous'). Do you know Abraham saw two grandchildren? Abraham lived to see Jacob and Esau reach the age of 15 before he died. When Abraham saw that Jacob and Esau were born, was Abraham surprised? No. But does the absence of the surprise keep one from enjoying the reality? No. We can be given a witness that something is going to happen; and yet it doesn't mean that when it does happen that we won't be thrilled.

In John 11, Jesus knew in a few minutes that Lazarus would be raised from the dead. But do you think that when he did it, he didn't enjoy seeing it? Of course he enjoyed it! God rejoices with us as things happen. So we can be given assurance that something is going to happen, and when it does how thrilling it is. I told you in the previous chapter about the two ladies that prayed for revival in the Hebrides, who were together given a vision of the church filled to overflowing, and very soon afterwards it was fulfilled. I am sure it thrilled them to see it happen.

Multiply

Abraham could see that God was serious about everything that he had said the first time. Do you know God's word is so literally fulfilled that I honestly believe, when we get to heaven, there will be streets of gold. I believe the fire of hell is literal. I know that sometimes the Bible can speak metaphorically, allegorically, and it could be that is the way we are supposed to understand heaven. But I know this, that when the Spirit is present in power, the Bible has a way of seeming so real, so powerful, that we are amazed at the simplicity and the literalness of it.

What did God say to Abraham? 'Your offspring will be like the sand by the seashore'—that's a lot of people. Count the stars! There are millions of them. This is what happened: the content of the oath was the same as the promise, but it brought out how literal it was. 'Multiplying I will multiply you.' How could Abraham feel multiplication?

This powerful internal witness was in terms of a specific kind of blessing. The term *blessing* is a general term that can refer to health, prosperity, and so on. But *multiplying* is specific, because it refers to numbers. What God did was that he narrowed the general term to refer to numbers.

But there was more: in Genesis 22, we can see more of the original vow, or oath (the writer of Hebrews doesn't quote it all). The first thing we notice in Genesis 22:17 is the *quantity* of the blessing: like the sand. Then there is the *quality* of the blessing: 'Your descendants will take possession of the cities of their enemies.'

There are two things to be seen here, in terms of the quality of the blessing. First, *the power to overcome the enemies*: 'Your descendants will take possession of the cities of their enemies.' This was seen when Jesus said to Peter, 'On this rock I will build my church and the gates of hell shall not overcome it.' That was the promise that God would ensure—while the church grew in number, there would be a built-in protection. So we have, by being the children of Abraham, not only the blessing of multiplication, but the blessing of this protection.

But there was more. In verse 18 of Genesis 22, 'and through your offspring all nations on earth will be blessed, because you have obeyed me.' That means that God has promised to his church *influence in the world*. Remember that when Abraham received this blessing, there was only Abraham and his son, Isaac; only two people at the time involved. But here we are at nearly the end of the twentieth century; how many people make up the church? Where would history be today without the church? Where would Britain be today without the church? Where would the United States be today without the church? If you look at the nations into which the gospel has penetrated, watch what happens to those nations. Wherever the gospel goes, something happens to the whole nation. It goes back to this oath that God swore to Abraham. It was a blessing not only of quantity, but of quality. We today have lived to see how this is true.

In Hebrews 6:15, the writer says that Abraham received what he wanted: 'And so, after waiting patiently, Abraham received what was promised.' The Greek word literally means 'and in this manner'. It is like saying, This is the way it was.

Abraham received what he wanted. When did he get it? Not in Haran, back before he came to Canaan; not in Egypt, where he and Sarah went; but it was after he tried to sacrifice Isaac. And the writer simply says, After waiting patiently.

When we get to heaven, we can ask Abraham: 'What was it like? Tell us, Abraham, what was it like, patiently waiting?' I believe Abraham will reply, 'If you knew how many times I said, How long, Lord?' Maybe you are like that, and you say, 'I have been serving the Lord for so many years and I have wanted this and I've wanted that, and I say, Lord, how long?' I promise you Abraham went through that. He was no superhuman, he was an ordinary man. But after he patiently endured, a day actually came. It was a date in history, it was a place on the map when Abraham was given leave to see the heavens opened, and God swore in his mercy; and according to the writer, that is called 'obtaining the promise'.

There is a clarification that is needed here. It is the Greek word, *epitukon*, it is the aorist tense of a word that means 'to acquire, to obtain'. It is a very rare word, only used five times in the New Testament. I don't know exactly what the word means but I can show you how it is used elsewhere.

In Romans 11:7: 'What Israel sought so earnestly it did not *obtain*, but the elect did.' In James 4:2: 'You kill and covet, but you cannot have what you *want*.' In Hebrews 11:33: 'Who through faith conquered kingdoms, administered justice, and *gained* what was promised.'

According to this same writer, when he uses it in Hebrews 11:33, there were those people in the Old Testament who obtained promises. We have seen what that means.

Do you know about Hezekiah? Hezekiah was told, 'You are going to die, get ready.' But Hezekiah cried, 'I don't want to die now,' and he just wept before the Lord. God said to him, 'I have seen your tears and I am going to add to your life fifteen years.' But Hezekiah said, 'Well, Isaiah, that's very good that you say it, thank you very much, and I believe that you are a good man. But I need to know that God said I was going to live fifteen years.' If you turn to 2 Kings 20:8-11, you will read:

> Hezekiah had asked Isaiah, 'What will be the sign that the LORD will heal me and that I will go up to the temple of the LORD on the third day from now?' Isaiah answered, 'This is the LORD's sign to you that the LORD will do what he has promised: Shall the shadow go forward ten steps, or shall it go back ten steps?' 'It is a simple matter for the shadow to go forward ten steps,' said Hezekiah. 'Rather, have it go back ten steps.' Then the prophet Isaiah called upon the LORD, and the LORD made the shadow go back the ten steps it had gone down on the stairway of Ahaz.

It was something that God did so supernaturally that Hezekiah says, 'Now I believe it.' He obtained the promise. It is the same as God swearing in his mercy.

A possible contradiction

In Hebrews 11:39 there is the expression, 'These were all commended for their faith, yet none of them received what had been promised.' Sometimes people give the impression they contradict themselves, and preachers are the worst in the world for that. However, some even accuse the Bible of contradicting itself. Verse 33 says these people obtained promises by faith, and then verse 39 says, 'none of them received what had been promised'. What is the explanation?

The first answer is that it is a different Greek word in verse 39 from that in verse 33. The other answer is that in verse 39, the promise is of Jesus' coming. I dare say the difference between obtaining the promise in verse 33 and receiving the promise in verse 39 is that verse 33 is talking about internal blessing, and verse 39 is talking about external blessing. Verse 33 is when Abraham received such a definite word from the Lord that he said, 'Now I believe it, I'll never doubt.' In verse 39, they were still waiting for the Messiah to come, the external blessing.

Hebrews 6:16-17 illustrates all that we have seen so far with regard to the promise and the oath: 'Men [he's speaking generally now] swear by someone greater than themselves, and the oath confirms what is said and puts an end to all argument'. All of us need to appeal to a higher authority in order to gain credibility.

Jesus had an alternative concept to offer in the Sermon on the Mount (Matt. 5:33-37):

> Again, you have heard that it was said to the people long ago, 'Do not break your oath, but keep the oaths you have made to the Lord.' But I tell you, Do not swear at all: either by heaven, for it is God's throne; or by the earth, for it is his footstool; or by Jerusalem, for it is the city of the Great King. And do not swear by your head, for you cannot make even one hair white or black. Simply let your 'Yes' be 'Yes' and your 'No,' 'No'; anything beyond this comes from the evil one.

Let's deal with this at a practical level for a moment. Is it right for a Christian to take the oath, to raise his right hand in a court of law, put his hand on the Bible and so forth? In my view, it is legitimate. I would even say that that is assumed by Hebrews 6:16, where we have just read how the writer says that men truly swear by the greater. He just assumed that is something that happens and he didn't say there was anything wrong with it at all.

I would say there are times when it is necessary, even in court. A believer may go to the judge and say, 'I happen to be a Christian. I don't need to take the oath.' The judge has a right to say, 'Then you don't have anything to worry about, do you? Why would you be afraid?' So, I believe that the Christian has nothing to hide when he is called upon to swear.

What, then, about Jesus' statement, when he said, Swear not at all? The reason for it was to show the way the third commandment of the Mosaic law was to be understood. Moses said, 'You shall not misuse the name of the LORD your God.' Now that can refer to cursing and using God's name in that way. But if a person thinks that is the only way the commandment is broken, he or she is quite wrong. Breaking the third commandment is one of the easiest things in the world to do, and people don't realise they are doing it.

Take the example of a preacher who, in order to back his interpretation of an issue, can bring God in and be so sure that he has God on his side. It is my duty, God helping me, never to superimpose my personal view upon the text. Much less to bring God's name in by saying, 'God has revealed this to me, therefore you must agree with me'. That would be abusing his name. The text must speak for itself and I am under the judgment of the word. Do you see what I mean? So this is the point Jesus was making in the Sermon on the Mount. It had nothing whatever to do with swearing in a court or anything like that.

Remember how James addressed those wealthy Christians who hired poor Christians to work for them, and then held back their wages. The poor Christians were defenceless and they cried out to the Lord Almighty (Jas. 5:1-6). James first rebuked these rich Christians for withholding the wages of the poor ones. But then he addressed the poor Christians and he says (vv. 7-11):

Be patient, then, brothers, until the Lord's coming. See how the farmer waits for the land to yield its valuable crop and how patient he is for the autumn and spring rains. You too, be patient and stand firm, because the Lord's coming is near. Don't grumble against each other, brothers, or you will be judged. The Judge is standing at the door!

Brothers, as an example of patience in the face of suffering, take the prophets who spoke in the name of the Lord. As you know, we consider blessed those who have persevered. You have heard of Job's perseverance and have seen what the Lord finally brought about. The Lord is full of compassion and mercy.

James was reminding these wronged believers, 'Do you know, you have a chance to be elevated to the level of the prophets?' So he gave the example of Job. What James does is, that having rebuked the wealthy Christians for withholding wages, he goes to the poor Christians who have been mistreated and he warns them lest they say, 'God's on our side and he's going to get you.' For the last thing James wrote in that section was:

Above all, my brothers, do not swear at all—not by heaven or by earth or by anything else. Let your 'Yes' be 'Yes', and your 'No , 'No', or you will be condemned.

In other words, he is warning these Christians who were the workers in the fields, who had been so mistreated by wealthy Christians. It would be so easy for them, especially now that James has come along and said, 'I'm with you,' to turn around and say to their wealthy masters, 'James is with us! What do you think of that?' But James says, 'If you do that, you will be condemned by God, because God does not take sides.' Believers never have the right to hold a grudge against anybody, and according to James, the worst thing to do is to bring God into it, and claim, 'He's with us!' James says,' Don't do it, because if you do, you are going to miss the blessing.'

So the principle is: we free God to be himself. If two Christians, concerned about the same problem, after prayer and searching the Scriptures, come to different conclusions, each is not to accuse the other of not following the Lord. If they do, both have broken the third commandment by bringing God into it. How do you think God feels, hearing both of them? We show our greatest adoration for God when we release him and do not bring his name into our little enterprise, and at the end of the day let him speak for himself. And if we give him time, he makes things clear, and this is why we have to wait on him. This is the reason James said, 'Wait. Be patient! There is coming a day when you workers in the field will be recompensed. But in the meantime, if you start getting bitter and holding a grudge, you will forfeit the blessing that could be yours.'

So exactly the same principle of Matthew 5:33-37 is found in James 5:12. It has nothing to do with a court of law.

And yet when God himself swears an oath to us we see clearly his opinion. Moreover, it is then we will feel little need to prove ourselves—we are set free to let God be himself. After all, the swearing of the oath means that God has taken over in any case.

22

Loving God Just Like He Is

Because God wanted to make the unchanging nature of his purpose very clear to the heirs of what was promised, he confirmed it with an oath. God did this so that, by two unchangeable things in which it is impossible for God to lie, we who have fled to take hold of the hope offered to us may be greatly encouraged (Hebrews 6:17-18).

In our study of Hebrews 6, we have noticed that one of the writer's emphases is that those Hebrew Christians should experience for themselves what he calls 'full assurance'. Today, it is sometimes called the *baptism of the Spirit* or the *sealing of the Spirit*. It can also be called God's rest, his swearing to us in grace.

I remember, many years ago, when I experienced this I thought I had discovered something new, and the doctrines that it led me to I thought no one had ever seen before! All that had happened was that I was led right into the main stream of historic Christian faith. And what I have also come to see is that what the writer calls 'full assurance' is what many of God's people in the Old and the New Testament have themselves come into. I wish that every Christian automatically came into this. I don't think that is the case, but in a sense it should be, because it is promised. What the writer does is tell us what Abraham himself experienced when God intervened in a way that he never had done before in Abraham's life; that is, he interposed an oath.

The Revised Standard Version translates 'confirmed it by an oath' as *'interposed* with an oath', the correct translation as it is the only time the Greek word is found in the New Testament, and it literally means 'interposed' or 'intervened'. It means God stepped in, and that is so with any oath of God, it is when he steps in. That's what happened with Abraham when he tried to sacrifice Isaac. God just stepped in. Up to then, as we have said, it was promise after promise, until one day God stepped in. God, who wanted to show the unchanging nature of his promise, interposed it by his oath.

A surprising experience

The interesting thing is that Abraham wasn't expecting it. I think, I can't say for sure, that to those who have experienced this it came as a complete surprise. We read accounts of experiences of famous Christians, and in so many cases they tell it was after a crisis that God became so real to them in a way they had never dreamed possible. From personal knowledge, those that I have talked to, who have gone through this experience, have testified that it was preceded by a kind of crisis, maybe some suffering, some unusual kind of adversity, which drove them to prayer. This is a frequent situation. I want to encourage you, should you find yourself in a crisis when you don't understand what is happening, and you are disillusioned, bewildered and tempted to despair.

Louise and I once attended a Prayer Breakfast where we heard Bishop Bill Burnett from South Africa give a wonderful address in which he explained that he had been converted as a child when he was in school; but in 1972, when he was praying he was filled with the Spirit, and Jesus Christ became so real to him. I can't be sure how old he was then, but he'd been a bishop since 1956.

By the way he described the experience and all that accompanied it, I knew exactly what he meant. In some cases God can give it to a young Christian, and sometimes to a person as they get older. But it is so real, it is so wonderful. I am not referring to anything fanatical; it is not wildfire, it is not phoney but it is absolutely real. Jesus Christ becomes so real.

Such people read the Bible with a certain fearlessness. Let me make clear what I mean by that. Do you know the feeling of reading the Bible defensively? It is when you read the Bible and think,' I don't like the way it is sounding, I don't think I believe this, or, I don't like that.' We have all had that happen to us, but what this experience of God does is, rather than being defensive, one just says, 'Well now, what *does* this mean? This is interesting, I want to get to the bottom of this.'

This is really how I myself came to a knowledge of Calvinism. I hadn't been taught it at all, and I would go to my professor and say, 'Look what I have found in the Bible.'

Then I would read a verse, and he would say, 'Well now, you're going off into Calvinism.'

I'd say, 'No, this is the Bible!'

'Yes, I know about that verse, but you had better be careful, you know that's one of the Calvinists' favourite proof texts.'

I said, 'Hold it! This is God's word. You tell me what it means.'

'Well, give me a little time on that.'

That was over thirty years ago! He still writes to me once or twice a year. The point is, we don't need to be afraid of any verse.

That's what happens when God interposes the oath. Promises for many, many years, then the oath.

God wants to bless us

Now verse 16, as we saw in the previous chapter, tells us what the oath does: it puts an end to all argument. Verse 17 tells us why God did it, for whom he did it and in what manner.

> Because God wanted to make the unchanging nature of his purpose *very clear* to the heirs of what was promised, he confirmed it with an oath.

Let's look at the way and manner of God's demonstration. The NIV simply says, *Because God wanted*. The Greek is trying to show how deeply God feels about it. The best way I can put it is that it is describing *God's tenderness*. Have you ever come to experience the tenderness of God? I think one of the hardest things for us to accept sometimes, is what nonetheless is absolutely true, that God wants to bless us far more than we want to be blessed.

You may want to quarrel with that statement. You may say, 'Well, Lord, I certainly do want you to bless me; why aren't you blessing me? Come on, Lord, if R.T. is right, he says you want to bless me more than I want to be blessed. Come on, do it!' In Ephesians 3:20 Paul says that God 'is able to do immeasurably more than all we ask or imagine', but he also adds, 'according to his power that is at work within us'.

God tests our love for him. Although we can say with words, 'God, I want you to bless me', God wants more than our words. He wants us to show fidelity to him in times when maybe we don't feel particularly worshipful, say when we are not in church. It is easy at the end of a service to bow and say, 'God, I give you my life again.' On such occasions we are feeling very intense, we are wanting to be closer to God, he is real to us then, and we feel good. But on Tuesday afternoon, we face a sudden temptation, and we give in to it; or there is an opportunity to show forgiveness but we hold a grudge instead and grieve the Holy Spirit. The fact is, in the church service, we just wanted God to act because in a moment of feeling emotional we said, 'God, I want you to bless me.'

The truth is, he wants to bless us. But it is through *endurance*, as when Abraham, in his trial of sacrificing Isaac, didn't know that when he passed the test he was going to experience a power of God greater than anything he had yet seen in his life. We never know when we are being tested. It could be in the most insignificant moment that we are being tested, when we say God isn't noticing this, God is taking no notice of me. We may be riding on the bus, walking down the street, reading a paper, but we are being tested. Maybe someone has been unkind to you at the office and you are plotting how to get even instead of showing forgiveness and love. All these things show how much we really want to be blessed.

But I am telling you, God does want to bless us more than we want him to. Think of those words of Jesus: 'It is the Father's good pleasure to give you the kingdom' (Luke 12:32). And I can tell you, God is faithful. Look at all that Job experienced (and Job couldn't have known how he was being tested), and the way he was accused by his friends, 'Job, there's got to be some sin in your life; there's no way all this could be happening to you otherwise.' There were times when Job sinned greatly by his self-righteousness, by his being opinionated. For until God came and answered out of the whirlwind, Job had it all figured out. But then Job said, 'I put my hand on my mouth.' And when Job prayed for his friends, the Lord turned everything into blessing.

God wants to bless us and we need to see that it is according to the power that works in us. God cannot deny himself.

For whom is all of this?

The writer says, *the heirs of the promise*. Who are these? Some say, Well that surely is *the Jews*. But the answer is, the heirs of the promise simply means *believers*. What Abraham learned on the day he tried to sacrifice Isaac, was that from then on, the offspring of Abraham would have continuity through the ages by regeneration, not procreation. Let me give an illustration.

Here is Abraham, and then Isaac, and then Jacob, and then the Twelve Tribes and so forth. Now, if the continuity is simply at the natural level, then we would have to say that the Seed of Abraham is continued simply by procreation. What Abraham had to learn was that God had to step in himself. When Abraham was willing to kill Isaac, and then received him back, he learned the great lesson that the seed of Abraham would be continued by God stepping in each time.

Isaac had to learn for himself that God is sovereign and on the throne. So did Jacob. Isaac had two sons, the elder, Esau, and the younger, Jacob, and normally this would mean that Esau automatically was going to be the seed of Isaac and Abraham. But God stepped in and showed that Jacob was the spiritual offspring of Abraham. It was not by procreation, each one had to have a conversion experience. That's the key. And the continuity of the seed to this very day is not by procreation, but by regeneration. Each person must experience conversion. That is what is meant by heirs of the promise.

The heirs are all those who believe. So if you have believed that God sent his Son into the world to die on the cross for your sins, and you transfer all hope in yourself over to what Jesus did for you on the cross, that makes you an heir of the promise. You are a believer and it means that you are a child of Abraham. God has stepped in and has given you faith sovereignly by his Spirit.

Why did he interpose the oath?

The answer: to show the *unchanging nature of his purpose*. What exactly does this mean? Three things:

First, it refers to *God's decree*, his sovereign will which goes back to before the foundation of the world and includes what God decreed from all eternity. We need to realise that all that God is doing today is no afterthought. Your own conversion was not an accident. I have heard people give their testimony and say, 'I just happened to walk into church, and if I hadn't done that I never would have been converted.' I know what they mean by that, and I don't dismiss the validity of their testimony, but the other side of the coin is that God brought them into the church, God brought them to the place where they heard the gospel. We do ourselves no favour to avoid this—to know it is a great mystery, that our own conversion was planned before the foundation of the world. It is no accident that we have been saved, it is a part of the unchanging nature of his purpose.

Secondly, it refers to *God's wisdom*. The 'unchanging nature of his purpose' simply means that God has infinite intelligence. This should be taken for granted, but I don't know of anything that is more thrilling than to discover all over again how intelligent God is. As Romans 11:33 puts it, 'How unsearchable his judgments, and his paths beyond tracing out!' Ephesians 1:8 tells us that all God has lavished on us was with 'all wisdom and understanding'.

Consider the intelligence of God in making the world: just look at nature, look at a rose, take the human body, or just look at the eye. What goes into the making of the eye, the intelligence behind it? Do you know all of the intelligence that God put into making nature, a flower, the human body, is what is behind his whole purpose in redemption, the intelligence whereby everything is perfectly done? For God, from the foundation of the world, determined to do everything in such a way that it could never be improved upon.

Look at your own life. Where were you ten years ago? Can you remember? Maybe you were dreading how this or that would turn out. Now you can see how God led you, and you could not have conceived of it being the way it worked out. He does beyond what we ask or think. We try to outguess him and we figure how he is going to do something, but his ways are past finding out. Infinite intelligence, and we see it in the way he guides our lives.

Thirdly, it refers to *consistency*. By consistency I mean that God does not decide later that he was wrong about something. We all make mistakes, and all of us, if we could start all over again, would live our lives differently. But with God, the unchanging nature of his purpose means that he does not make mistakes. What he has decreed to do was exactly right. His wisdom is unimproveable. And so he is consistent. This means that each of us has been dealt with in such a way that God wouldn't change anything.

This also means that his promise stays the same. I know of some people who join the church but later show they haven't really been converted. They give the church a few months; maybe they were in some kind of trouble, a medical problem, or a problem at work, or whatever, and they decided they needed religion, so they come into the church; they are all excited, and people are rejoicing that they seem to have been converted. But after a few months they get bored.

What bores them? The precise thing that turns the rest of us on—just to hear the same gospel again and again. The proof that you are converted is that when you hear the gospel you just love it all over again. It is like being converted again. When you hear the gospel you are thrilled.

So if a person gets bored with the gospel they betray they have not really had a conversion experience. Because when God meets with us, he brings us back to the same old truth. When the Holy Spirit comes to the church in revival, it is a restoration of the same old gospel. He will never repudiate what the church has held to in the past: what Athanasius saw back in the fourth century—Jesus is very God of very God, light of light; what Luther saw—the great truth of justification by faith; when the church is revived they see that is just the way it is.

So there is in God this consistency: God does not decide later that he was wrong about this or that.

We then have these two immutable things or two unchangeable acts: the *promise* and the *oath*. (The Living Bible is a modern translation that makes this explicitly clear.) In the Greek the word for acts is *pragmaton*, from which we get the word, *pragmatic*. It is literally two acts. For when God promised, he was acting. Nothing changed in all those promises. When God would come to Abraham time and time and time again, he was acting, but it was always the same.

But then comes the oath. Is it different? Is the content of the oath different? Not at all. Do you know, it is the same thing exactly. Well then, why have it? The answer is, because it makes things plainer. Instead of being on the back row, you're on the front row. When it comes to seeing God work, God brings you right to the centre of the front row as it were, and you can see everything close up, everything is so plain and so real. That's the difference. It is the difference between seeing God far off and seeing him close at hand.

God is truth

But the writer adds something with regard to these two things: whether it be the promise or the oath *it is impossible for God to lie*. Now to me, this is the most wonderful thing of all about God, that he cannot lie. Why can't he lie? Because he is truth, and he cannot deny himself.

There is something here I want you to see. It is not that God chose not to lie. That would be to miss it entirely. We may be in a position where we say, 'I'm going to tell the truth about this, I choose to tell the truth no matter how much it hurts.' We are in a position to be like that because we came from our mothers' wombs with a sinful nature and we are tempted to lie. We are often tempted to cover up this or deviate from that or not have to say everything about something else. And so we say, 'I choose to be honest, I choose to tell the truth.'

But that's not the case with God. He cannot do anything but tell the truth because his nature is truth. By nature he is honest. He has integrity. He cannot do anything but speak truth. I repeat, it is not that he chooses to be truthful, he *is* truthful, and he can't be anything else.

I wonder if you have ever had this happen to you: it has happened to me a few times. When I felt the presence of God very near, I could see what God was like, and I felt so relieved that God is *just like he is*. Then the thought crossed my mind, 'Isn't it wonderful that God is like that?' What if it were otherwise? There is nothing we could do about it. In other words, if he wasn't what he was, because he is God, we'd have to take it. And to think that our God *is* just what he is! Has that ever gripped you? What if he were other than he is?

Take a country ruled by a tyranny, where they know nothing but oppression. What if God were like that? Let me say this: the Devil is like that; he keeps people afraid, and motivates them by fear. But God is purest love. To think that the God we have is all good, that he is honest, he is truthful, he keeps his word.

Why is the writer emphasising this point? He's letting us know that if we will seek the Lord with all our heart, we will find him in this wonderful way. He is not mocked. What Jesus called life more abundant, can be ours.

23

The Comfort of God

God did this so that, by two unchangeable things in which it is impossible for God to lie, we who have fled to take hold of the hope offered to us may be greatly encouraged. We have this hope as an anchor for the soul, firm and secure. It enters the inner sanctuary behind the curtain, where Jesus, who went before us, has entered on our behalf. He has become a high priest for ever, in the order of Melchizedek (Hebrews 6:18-20).

Why did God give the oath? That we might be greatly encouraged. After all, that is what growing Christians want—to know God in this profound, lucid, intimate manner. For those reading this who do not have what the writer calls 'full assurance of faith', is this what you want? I certainly hope so. The writer wanted it for those to whom he wrote the letter. If there is anyone who does not have this blessing, you can take one of two attitudes: first, negative—saying, 'I don't think there's anything to it. I've got it all.' You are hostile to the very idea. The other attitude is, 'Oh, how much indeed I want this.' And it is to such that the writer is saying, There is great encouragement (NIV) or strong consolation (AV).

The writer uses the Greek word, *paraklesin*, very similar to *paracletos*. Now what is the point? Jesus said to his disciples in the Upper Room, 'I am going to go away, but I am going to send another Comforter,' another *paracletos*, the Holy Spirit in other words. Sometimes the Holy Spirit is referred to by Christians as the Paraclete. This word is very like the one that is used in this verse, Hebrews 6:18. In 2 Corinthians 1:3-7, this word is used nine times:

Praise be to the God and Father of our Lord Jesus Christ, the Father of compassion, and the God of all *comfort*; who *comforts* us in all our troubles, so that we can *comfort* those in any trouble with the *comfort* we ourselves have received from God. For just as the sufferings of Christ flow over into our lives, so also through Christ our *comfort* overflows. If we are distressed, it is for your *comfort* and salvation; if we are *comforted*, it is for your *comfort*, which produces in you patient endurance of the same sufferings we suffer. And our hope for you is firm, because we know that just as you share in our sufferings, so also you share in our *comfort*.

What the writer is saying is that the fact that God made the oath to Abraham provides *us* with a strong consolation. Now the difference then between the two words is that this 'comfort' (*parakleson*) is based upon the promise, whereas *paracletos* is the very presence of God. So we receive consolation from knowing that God said it. But what Jesus meant when he said, 'I will send you another Comforter,' was the fact that the Holy Spirit would come to live in believers and give them the comfort by his very presence.

Who qualifies for this comfort?

Those who have fled for refuge. What does *to flee* mean? It simply means to run, to make an escape. What we have here is a word that implies running from something, trying to escape something.

What is it that we are escaping from? Well, what did John the Baptist say? 'Flee from the coming wrath.' This is one way of saying it. We are hoping through the promise that the wrath of God will in no way catch up with us. So the Christian is one who has fled from the wrath of God.

This presupposes a U-turn. We were walking towards destruction and then we were made aware of God's wrath, and we made a 180 degree turn and are now running in the opposite direction.

We who want to rediscover God are therefore admonished to

flee from the possibility of a Hebrews 6:6 situation as the non-Christian is warned to flee from God's wrath. The possibility of God swearing in his wrath should spur us on to a greater repentance. We do not have the fear of going to hell (because we are saved), but we should fear his swearing in wrath none the less!

We would do well to look again at the fundamental truth, What is a Christian? The parallel truth, then, is this: we should take hold of the hope offered to us with the same godly fear that motivated us to flee to Christ in the first place.

The reality of Hell

It is important that we see this, for it presupposes the writer's view of God's wrath and eternal punishment. Why did God send his Son into the world? If you ever are tempted to question the doctrine of eternal punishment and everlasting hell, all you need do is come to terms with why Jesus died on the cross. If there is no hell, there was no need for Jesus to die on the cross. If God wasn't angry with sin, and mankind for sinning, there was no point. It is a reminder that the Christian faith is based upon the premise that there is a heaven and a hell.

Why is this important? Well, the danger is of having a flabby kind of Christianity that would encourage conversions on the basis of, 'Well, you're going to be better off in this life if you become a Christian.' Most testimonies that we hear today, and I am not saying that these testimonies are insincere, are taken up with the idea that things have been so much better for me since I have become a Christian. I am not denying that is true, and yet, if that is why a person decides to become a Christian, I question in a way whether they have really been converted. I am not saying a person cannot be, because in the gospel we have many ways of people being converted; there is more than one way of a person coming to realise that he or she needs a Saviour. But this is my point: the Christian faith presupposes that God sent his Son into the world because God was angry with the world. Yes, he loved the world, but he hates sin, and right after John 3:16, comes '... whoever does not believe stands condemned already because he has not believed in the name of God's one and only Son' (John 3:18). The reason that Jesus came to die is 'that whoever believes in him shall not perish.'

Remember, the reason we ran to Christ is because we were convicted of our sin, and we knew things were not right between us and God. It was an angry God we faced, and we were forced to flee. But we would never flee from something unless we were made to. A quote from Calvin's comments on this verse is interesting: 'We do not fly for refuge to God without being forced thereby.' We had come to the place where we had no choice. Once we saw the wrath of God, we started running.

This will have a profound effect upon the way we see things. There is no sense of, 'How fortunate the Church is now I've come into it'; 'Well, God is going to be much better off now that I have become a Christian.' The modern attitude is that people do God some kind of favour when they walk inside a church. They want to do something for God. But that's not a Christian. The Christian is one who is running from the wrath of God.

The analogy here, in a sense, is Numbers 35, where there is the account of the cities of refuge. A city of refuge was the place to which a person who had killed someone accidentally might flee. The person who found this city of refuge might say, 'I am here because nobody else will have me, I am on the run.' There is no kind of a sense of worth, that that city was privileged to have him! An accidental killer would not arrive and say, 'Well, you all need me, I can see.' Oh no! There is no sense of personal self-esteem. That is the point here in Hebrews 6:18.

We are all in the church because God boxed us into a corner. There was no choice. This is a good way to tell whether you have been converted; do you see yourself as a hell-deserving sinner?

Christians indebted to God

Christians will be indebted to God for the rest of their lives and throughout eternity for two things. First, because they saw the impending wrath. Others don't see it until they find themselves swallowed up in it, but it is too late to escape then. The difference

between the Christian and the non-Christian is that the Christian
was given advance warning, believed the message, and he flew
for refuge. There are two sorts of non-Christian—those who
hear the message and don't believe it, and those who haven't
heard it. Why it is that there will be some who perish who never
heard the gospel is not a question I can answer. I don't understand
it and yet I know of no comfort that can be given for those who
have not heard the gospel. But we who are converted can take no
credit for being saved.

Secondly, we had a place to go to. Jesus said, 'Come to me,
all you who are weary and burdened, and I will give you rest'
(Matt. 11:28). A Christian never gets over being saved, and will
never get over it. I don't know why God saved me; I may never
know. I may never understand it. All I can do is thank him. I am
reminded of the words of C. T. Studd, 'If Jesus Christ be God and
died for me, no sacrifice can be too great for me to make for him.'

Why else do we flee? To *take hold of the hope offered to us*.
The Greek word for 'take hold' literally means 'to seize', to
grasp something that is, as it were, under your control. I don't
mean that we are going to control God or anything like that, but
the point the writer makes in using this word is that we know we
have got *it*, the hope.

The anchor of the soul

What is that hope that is offered to us? It is the future and the
present; it is heaven, and a little bit of heaven to go to heaven on.
What is it to lay hold of the hope set before us? It is to know
beyond any doubt whatever that it is ours. We may know it by
the simple promise: 'Come to me, all you who are weary and
burdened, and I will give you rest.' We know what we are fleeing
from; we know where we are heading, and we know that we will
not be refused. Why? The writer tells us. We already have it: 'We
have this hope as an anchor for the soul' (v. 19). The future
becomes present.

At this stage, the writer uses a metaphor, an anchor. (In the
early church the main signal that was passed to other Christians

was the sign of the fish. But there was another symbol—an anchor.) The function of the anchor is to remain fixed in the sea-bed whatever the conditions at sea; so the rougher the weather, the more important is the anchor for the stability and safety of the boat. So it was that the anchor was used graphically among early Christians.

W. H. Griffith-Thomas suggests that the 'figure may be taken from the practice that prevailed in old times in the harbours of the Mediterranean and other inland seas. In every harbour, as may be seen indeed to this day, was a great stone, and usually there were a number of such, immovably embedded in the ground near the water's edge. That rock, as we understand, was the anchoria (the Greek is *agkura*, which is our word here by the way). It served ordinarily as a mooring for vessels in those days. But it also had another function. Sometimes the ship could not by the means of its sails, make its way to a secure mooring within the harbour. In such a case, a forerunner would go ashore in a small boat with a line, which would be made fast to the anchoria, that was sure and steadfast, being of ample strength and immovably embedded in the ground. Therefore, those on the ship had only to hold fast to the line, and by means of it, and by patience, draw near to the shore.'

Some have speculated whether the writer of Hebrews was a seaman in some sense. The person who used this metaphor knew what it was to be at sea and the importance of having an anchor that would hold in a time of great storm, for the anchor determined the safety of the boat and the passengers.

What the writer says here is that believers have an anchor of the soul. Where do you suppose the anchor has been set down? In the Old Testament image that we are being directed to by the writer, it is in the most holy place, called the Holy of Holies, inside which was the Ark of the Covenant, known as the Mercy Seat. To get there, the High Priest had to go through a curtain or veil. The writer tells us that this anchor of the soul is inside the veil. We know that we cannot ever be lost because Jesus entered into the most holy place, into heaven and so we are secure.

The priestly work of Christ

The theme of the priestly work of Christ is certainly central to the letter to the Hebrews. The writer first introduced the subject in chapter 2:17, he repeats it in 3:1, 4:14-15, and throughout chapter 5, and now at the conclusion of Hebrews 6 he says in verse 20, 'Where Jesus, who went before us, has entered on our behalf. He has become a high priest for ever, in the order of Melchizedek'. Earlier in chapter 5 he dealt with the problem of why these Hebrew Christians were not able to absorb all that they ought to be able to absorb on the question of Melchizedek, and he tells them why and he warns them. But now he returns to the subject of Melchizedek.

The priestly work of Christ essentially includes two things: the death of Christ, and the intercession of Christ. But another way to put it is this: the death of Christ is seen as an offering; the intercession of Christ as the application. In the Four Gospels the death of Christ is described. In the letter to the Hebrews, the references to the priestly work of Christ have largely to do with his intercession. The writer touched on the death of Christ in Hebrews 2:9—'he might taste death for everyone'—but in the main, Hebrews deals with the intercession of Christ.

Donald Guthrie, in his commentary on Hebrews, puts it like this: 'this hope is two things: an objective reality to be seized and a subjective reality to be experienced.' This will bear looking into, for verses 19-20 take in both these aspects. Objective reality is what is there, while subjective reality is what I feel is there. Subjective is what a person perceives to be true; objective is what is absolutely there.

The objective reality to be seized is the fact that Jesus has gone into the very presence of God. He is there. That's a fact. But what is the subjective reality to be experienced? We have this hope as an anchor of the soul, firm and secure.

When I studied at Oxford, I discovered what Calvin taught on this subject. He said that the death of Christ was an offering. This is the word he always used, and he likened it to what happened in public on the altar in the temple. But no atonement took effect until the high priest went behind the curtain, which he could only do once a year. That action was a picture of the application of the death of Christ. So the death of Jesus corresponds to the holy place where the sacrifice was offered and killed, but the blood goes into the most holy place. The point is, when Jesus cried with a loud voice and yielded up his spirit, the curtain in the temple was torn in two from top to bottom (Matt. 27:51).

Now, the writer tells us something very interesting. He says that the anchor that we have goes within the veil. Why does it hold firm and secure? Why is it sure? Why does it hold? The answer is because it is an objective reality. We believe that Jesus went to heaven.

But Jesus is called the forerunner (AV). It is the translation of a Greek word *prodomos* and this is the only time it is used in the New Testament. In such situations we have to go to either the Septuagint, the Greek translation of the Old Testament, or to ancient Hellenistic literature and see how the word was used there. How was *prodomos*, translated forerunner, used? It was literally a spy or scout, one who went before anybody else, a soldier who might go and explore something fully in advance of the whole army.

So what do we learn? Jesus is a forerunner, he has gone before us, and has experienced objectively what we some day will also experience. But subjectively we experience it now. Why? Because we believe it, and because it is just a part of our being, we believe it with all our hearts, that this anchor holds within the veil.

We may conclude two things concerning the Holy of Holies: firstly, it is the presence of God; secondly, it is the place where the atonement was ratified. The blood of the sacrifice was accepted then when it was sprinkled on the Mercy Seat.

Remember the illustration of a ship that could not get into the harbour, so a little boat went ahead and secured a rope and the big ship outside just held on to it. The people of God are seen as a ship at sea, while the forerunner has made it to the harbour. Therefore, we must say that Jesus has gone to where we are travelling. And so, in the meantime, where are we? We are in the open sea, and for a while we will experience the fury of the wind and the waves. Yet even in the storm we feel firm. Why? Because our anchor holds. It is inside the veil. So, if we wonder whether Jesus is really there, objectively we can't see him, but yet subjectively, we feel him and think, 'Well, it is so. It is so, because my heart witnesses.' As Calvin put it, 'It is a faith so sure that you know you won't be deceived.' People look at us and think we are crazy because we trust the Lord. Yet we know that we are not deceived.

Also our forerunner is seen as a *pledge* that we too shall go where he is. Someone has called it a link between the visible and the invisible. Remember how in the Temple only the high priest could go behind the curtain; when he did he became invisible and could not be seen by the onlookers. So with the intercession of Jesus. Nobody can see him intercede; it is invisible. Although people saw him die, no one can see him intercede.

The writer of Hebrews is the only writer of the New Testament to make this point (thank God for the letter to the Hebrews), for he knew that although Jesus had fulfilled all that the Old Testament pictured and predicted, he knew that more had to happen. This is why most of Hebrews is about the aspect of the application of the blood, and not the shedding of the blood. It is concerned mainly with the application, what goes on where it is invisible, in heaven itself, what nobody here can see.

Objectively there were people who knew that Jesus died on the cross, no one questioned that. Even the most cynical critics today will acknowledge that Jesus died on the cross. But what makes a person a Christian is not that he or she believes that Jesus died on the cross, but that Jesus was raised from the dead. But they believe more happened after his resurrection, that Jesus applies his blood in the most holy place.

Christ is our pledge. What's a pledge? Well that's something you can see, it is visible. This is why Calvin calls the bread and the wine in the Lord's Supper pledges of our election. The Lord's Supper brings the death of Christ before us and so when Calvin talked about the presence of Christ, he meant the spiritual

presence, not the superstitious view that the bread and the wine
literally become the body and blood of the Lord. Calvin said that
spiritually by faith the bread and the wine represent the pledge
that Jesus died, and by trusting his death, we know that we are
saved. But we also know that how we were saved is that the
blood that he shed was sprinkled in the most holy place. So the
writer says that we know that's where Jesus went. He entered
into heaven.

The writer says that Jesus is made a high priest in the order
of Melchizedek. Here's something very interesting. The Levitical
priesthood was of the order of Aaron. But there is one main
difference between the priesthood of Jesus and what Aaron
represented—Aaron died and Jesus lives for ever.

What has this to do with us who want to discover God all over
again? I answer, we never outgrow the gospel. We never
outgrow pleading for mercy, the stance we had to take when we
were converted. Our rediscovery of God will be experienced by
pleading for his mercy, by realising the merit of Christ's atoning
blood and by knowing that Jesus is at God's right hand—to grant
us a measure of the Holy Spirit beyond what we may have
imagined.

Conclusion

I hope by now you already feel an increased ease that the sober verses of Hebrews 6:4-6 do not describe you. In a word: if you are seriously worried, they don't!

But I now want to elaborate on my statement above. In this conclusion I want to offer practical help by which you can see for yourself: (i) that you are not among those who cannot be renewed again to repentance; and (ii) how you may be brought to the place, like Abraham, whereby God may well swear an oath in mercy to you.

I am often asked, do I know people that I believe are in a Hebrews 6:6 situation? Yes—I think. I would stop short of saying I know for sure. I do not have apostolic discernment as our writer had—or as Peter had when he spoke with authority to Ananias and Sapphira (Acts 5:1-11). But I have had grave concerns over some I have known.

Many years ago I knew a pastor in America who had been a godly man, who showed contempt for an astonishing move of the Spirit in his own church. He was present in a service where such power was present that a haze came into the very auditorium —a smoke so thick that one could not see across the large room. It was a service that changed the direction of my life —and his. He was never the same again; the spiritual-mindedness and insight that had characterised his preaching ended. He never changed his mind about this awesome service, neither was he brought to any noticeable repentance. What anointing he once had was gone. He later died a premature death. I believe he is in Heaven, but his usefulness here below after he spoke contemptuously of that service was minimal. Like King Saul, he continued for a while but his anointing was gone. Billy Graham said to a friend of mine that his greatest fear was that God would take his hand off him. That is my fear. I hope it is yours.

How then can we know—short of God swearing an oath to us—that we are not in that hopeless category of those who can never be renewed again to repentance?

1. Conviction of sin
When we are gripped with a sense of sin generally and specific sins particularly it proves that we are still on speaking terms with God—he is in fact speaking to us and we are hearing him. The initial work of the Spirit is to convict of sin, according to John 16:8. But this does not end there. What Isaiah experienced is what we all should experience continually as proof we are seeking the glory of God. When we become acutely conscious of sin, especially when grieving the Spirit, we may be sure that repentance is taking place.

2. Walking in the light
When we confess the sin that God has put his finger on—which comes as a result of walking in the light, we are cleansed (I John 1:7-9). If we say we have no sin we are deceived. Walking in the light shows that we have heard God —and obeyed. The Hebrew *shamar* means simultaneously to hear and obey. This is the only kind of hearing God recognises. 'If you hear my voice' means hearing so as to obey. That is walking in the light.

3. A tender conscience
This is why the writer warned, 'See to it, brothers, that none of you has a sinful, unbelieving *heart* that turns away from the living God' (Heb. 3:12). We must maintain a docile, warm heart. This is what David had. He was 'conscience-stricken' for having cut off a corner of Saul's robe—an act which might not have worried some. But it did David.

4. Being gripped by the word
When any word of God—whether by preaching or by reading the Bible—grips us it is a sure sign that God is dealing with us. It is an ominous sign that we are 'dull of hearing' when the case

is otherwise. We should treasure any moment when we are gripped by any part of God's word.

5. Openness to the Holy Spirit

On this point there would be few Christians who would deny being closed. Some think they are open to the Spirit merely because they have an orthodox doctrine of the Trinity generally and see the need of the Spirit particularly to convict people of sins. But I would have to say that is not enough. By 'openness to the Spirit' I mean a conscious welcoming and *expectancy* that the Spirit will witness to our minds and hearts directly and immediately. For example, one can be open to the word and assume that such is openness to the Spirit too. I doubt it. One must believe that the Spirit is willing to manifest himself today—not just in the earliest church—but as he did in the early church, say, to Philip (Acts 8). When one has not closed his mind to the Spirit dealing with us directly today but is truly expectant, one may know this is proof that he has not passed beyond hope. Those who cannot be renewed again to repentance have no such wish.

These five principles, then, may assure anyone that he has not reached stone deafness. That being true therefore, what then? Is your *only* concern that you are *not* in a Hebrews 6:6 situation? If so, you are still in danger. In other words, if that alone is your concern there lurks the possibility that you could still irretrievably backslide at some stage. Remember: failure to enter into God's rest and falling away ultimately come to the same thing. The failure to enter God's rest up to now does not mean one is in a Hebrews 6:6 situation; the promise 'still stands', but we must be careful that none of us 'be found to have fallen short of it' (Heb. 4:1).

Is there a guarantee that we will never, never, never be a candidate for Hebrews 6:6? There is. And that is to follow the seven principles outlined below. I can guarantee this; I will lay my reputation and integrity and all I believe on the line for this.

How to rediscover God

There are many expressions that convey what can be meant by rediscovering God. Some will want to call it 'the baptism of the Holy Spirit'. Dr Martyn Lloyd-Jones preferred the phrase 'sealing of the Spirit', which he regarded as the 'highest form of assurance'. The writer of the Epistle to the Hebrews uses several expressions, among them being 'full assurance', 'entering God's rest' or being given 'God's oath'.

We live in a day in which people are used to short cuts, fast food and quick service. Some bring this into the church and give the impression that God can be rediscovered in much the same way. I am not so sure. Mind you, God can do anything. He loves to offend the mind in order to reach the heart and he delights in using foolish things to confound the wise.

But to the person who is gravely serious about his quest to rediscover God I give seven principles that will lead one to a rediscovery of the word and Spirit—and which may also lead one to God's granting the oath to us as he swore to Abraham (Hebrews 6:13ff).

1. Be open to the truth that there is more of God for you than you now have.
I believe A. W. Tozer was right: you can have as much of God as you want. Some people are almost paranoid about any experience with God subsequent to conversion. They want to say that since we are 'in Christ' and thereby 'have it all' by merely being a Christian, anything beyond that is to undermine the gospel. I don't believe it. Those who are closed to having more of God run the risk of finally coming short of God's rest so as to become stone deaf to the Spirit. I therefore plead with you on bended knee, be open.

> No eye has seen,
> no ear has heard,
> no mind has conceived
> what God has prepared for those who love him (I Cor. 2:9).

This verse is a paraphrase of Isaiah 64:4 which in fact ends with 'those who wait for him'. That is not a reference to what Heaven will be like (even if the verse fits). For Paul continued: 'But God has revealed it to us by his Spirit' (I Cor. 2:10), which brings the realisation to the here and now!

2. Walk in all the light God gives you.

God does not lead us directly from A to Z but from A to B, B to C etc. It is one step at a time. What Jesus said to the disciples is also true with us: 'I have much more to say to you, more than you can now bear' (John 16:12). As I am obedient to the light that God has thrown upon my path I can be sure there will be more light. This light will reveal hidden sin of which I had not been aware, and with the conviction of sin comes duty. My frequent question is, 'Lord, why didn't you show that to me before now?' The answer is, obviously, I couldn't handle it before now.

We all like to think we are the exception. 'Yes, Lord, I will do all you say—tell me everything,' as if we could cope with it. But we can't. God gives us light in doses, in degrees. As we walk in the light we have an ever-increasing fellowship with God.

As long as I am walking in all the light I see, I may be sure that *at any moment* the blessing of the Holy Spirit will come —to exceed my greatest expectation!

3. Be thankful for the least blessing.

Jesus said, 'Whoever can be trusted with very little can also be trusted with much, and whoever is dishonest with very little will also be dishonest with much' (Luke 16:10). When we affirm the least thing God does in us he is honoured and glorified. He loves praise and gratitude. 'Do not be anxious about anything, but in everything, by prayer and petition, *with thanksgiving*, present your requests to God' (Phil. 4:6).

A few years ago I began a new practice in my private quiet time. I blush to think of the years preceding when I didn't do it— to take a few moments *every single day*, when I began to pray, to thank God for *everything* he did over the previous twenty-four hours. I literally thank him for everything. Every single thing I can think of. I keep a journal. I read yesterday's entries to remind me of the day. Almost always there are five or six things (sometimes more) which I enumerate with thanksgiving.

If we are thankful for that which is least, we will be thankful for the big things.

4. Do not underestimate the test God secretly has in mind that lies behind the suffering he allows for you.

We may pray for God to turn up in our lives but may not be prepared for the manner he chooses to do it! It is often through suffering. No suffering for the Christian is accidental; it comes by God's sovereign permission and with a definite purpose.

Any suffering. Great. Small. Losing your keys or a serious disease. When your feelings get hurt or if you lose your job. The withholding of vindication or the sudden disappointment.

> Every joy or trial
> Cometh from above,
> Traced upon our dial
> By the sun of love;
> We may trust him fully
> All for us to do –
> Those who trust him wholly
> Find him wholly true.   Francis Ridley Havergal

It is said of Hezekiah, 'God left him to test him and to know everything that was in his heart' (2 Chron. 32:31). God still does this sort of thing with his chosen vessels. It is a high compliment— a most high compliment. It means I can be trusted with this trial! I will therefore *dignify that trial* by refusing to complain or prematurely hastening its end.

Most unusual blessing follows a period of suffering (1 Pet. 5:10). That being true, then, I can take *any* suffering as reason to be expectant! The blessing I long for may be close at hand!

5. Seek God's face, not his hand, daily.

We live in the age of the 'me generation'. The health and wealth 'gospel' plays into our greed. There is little offence in the 'name it and claim it' theology. Why? It is almost totally seeking God's hand—asking him to do this or that for me.

God wants us to have intimacy with him. That comes by seeking his face. The blessing I am talking about is not with regard to material things—promotion, better job, possessions, or even healing. I am talking about rediscovering *God*—just to know him.

God's face is a symbol for his heart. When his face smiles on us it is because his heart is glad. He is pleased. This must be our supreme desire or all else I have said above will be nonsense to you.

Moreover, this must be done *daily*. I ask: how much time do you spend in prayer? The average church leader in Britain spends an average of four minutes a day. No wonder the church is powerless! Listen to these lines from Martin Luther: 'I have a very busy day today; I must spend not two, but three, hours in prayer.'

I ask the members of my own church to spend no fewer than thirty minutes a day alone with God. Every minister should spend twice that time. If you are serious about God, this will not be offensive to you but will cause your heart to leap.

6. Thank God that you are gripped by the truth, which proves that you are not in a Hebrews 6:6 situation.

When your heart is gripped by the word and the Spirit, be very thankful for this. Realise that it is by his sheer grace and that you therefore have obviously not reached that cut-off point of not being able to be renewed to repentance. The renewal of repentance is the lifeline to spiritual blessing that is described in 2 Corinthians 3:18. When you are gripped by the truth it is God at work; it proves he is on speaking terms with you.

You may also be aware of your unworthiness. Who among us has not given God good reason to wash his hands of us long ago? Be thankful. Bow to him.

A friend of mine was given a special word by a minister. It was: 'This too will pass, and the truth is worse than what they know.' With every crisis we tend to think, 'The worst has come—there will be no more opportunities.' But that is the devil. The devil, who knows the Bible backwards and forwards, will make you think that the sin you have committed makes you a Hebrews 6:6 candidate. Wrong. You *are* gripped by the word, are you not? That is God at work. What is more, the truth about you—which he knows—is worse than what others know.

It should make one feel very, very grateful. This coheres with what I said previously about being thankful. 'Hitherto has the Lord helped us.' He is at work; he won't desert you now. Be thankful. Tell him!

7. Learn to detect God's test by his playful provocation.
I have sometimes called it the 'Divine Tease', for that is exactly what God often does. It is when God appears to say or do something which he doesn't really mean! For example, on the road to Emmaus Jesus 'acted as if he were going further' (Luke 24:28). When Jesus walked on the lake with the disciples straining at the oars, 'he was about to pass by them' (Mark 6:48), when in fact he wanted them to cry out to him—which they did. Jesus said to Philip, 'Where shall we buy bread for these people to eat?' He asked this only to test him, for he already had in mind what he was going to do' (John 6:5b-6). It was the way Elijah treated Elisha—to see how much he wanted a double portion of his spirit (2 Kings 2:1-10). When God told Moses he would destroy his rebellious followers Moses interceded for them instead—which in fact is what God hoped Moses would do (Num. 14:11-19). When the angel said to Jacob, 'Let me go, for it is daybreak' he blessed Jacob for holding on (Gen. 32:26-29). Learn to detect God dealing with you like this!

When we tell God we want his blessing more than anything else it is as though he says, 'Really?' and tests us by putting obstacles in our way.

What I have been writing about is serious stuff. Do you want to rediscover God? *Do you really?* This rediscovery comes to those who love him and wait for him and desire the blessing of his Spirit more than anything else in the world. But it follows an earnest seeking of his face.

> So I say to you: Ask and it will be given to you; seek and you will find; knock and the door will be opened to you. For everyone who asks receives; he who seeks finds; and to him who knocks, the door will be opened. Which of you fathers, if your son asks for a fish, will give him a snake instead? .... If you then, though you are evil, know how to give good gifts to your children, how much more will your Father in heaven give the Holy Spirit to those who ask him? (Luke 11:9-11,13).

> You will seek me and find me when you seek me with all your heart (Jer. 29:13).

The Bible is God putting his integrity on the line. His honour is at stake. Are you then seeking him with all your heart? If so, it is the best possible state to be in.

Christian Focus Publications publishes biblically-accurate books for adults and children. The books in the adult range are published in three imprints.

Christian Heritage contains classic writings from the past.

Christian Focus contains popular works including biographies, commentaries, doctrine, and Christian living.

Mentor focuses on books written at a level suitable for Bible College and seminary students, pastors, and others; the imprint includes commentaries, doctrinal studies, examination of current issues, and church history.

For a free catalogue of all our titles, please write to
Christian Focus Publications,
Geanies House, Fearn,
Ross-shire, IV20 1TW, Great Britain

For details of our titles visit us on our web site
http://www.christianfocus.com